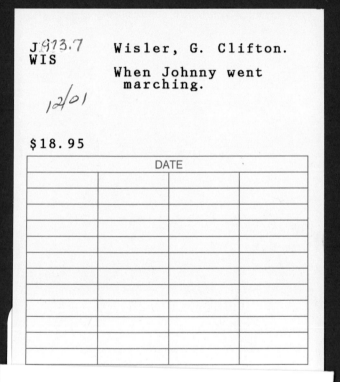

When Johnny Went Marching

The boys of Adams, Massachusetts, formed their own company, the Plunkett Zouaves. Armed with wooden rifles and dressed in the fashionable French style of many early Civil War regiments, they posed for this photograph early in the war. How many of these boys joined the fighting during the four years that followed is not known.

WHEN JOHNNY WENT MARCHING

YOUNG AMERICANS
FIGHT THE CIVIL WAR

G. Clifton Wisler

HarperCollins*Publishers*

We gratefully acknowledge permission to publish the following photographs in this book:

Alabama Department of History and Archives (93); Arkansas History Commission (28); Bardeen, *A Little Fifer's War Diary* (3);

Beyer and Keydel, *Deeds of Valor* (2, 25, 66); Eli Lilly Company (75); Emilio, *A Brave Black Regiment* (73); Illinois State Historical

Library (iii, 23, 32, 43, 44, 82); Library of Congress (21); Mike Miner (59); *Photographic History of the Civil War* (6, 19, 48, 78);

Proceedings of Twelfth Annual Meeting of the Society of the 28th Wisconsin Volunteer Infantry (55, 56); South Caroliniana Library,

University of South Carolina, Columbia (36); State Historical Society of Iowa in Iowa City, Iowa (5); U.S. Army Military History

Institute: Dorothy Craver Collection (64), Claudine Dollar Collection (30), Bill Elswick Collection (4), Gloucester County

Historical Society Collection (17), Professor Jay S. Hoar Collection (12), Massachusetts Commandery, MOLLUS (xii, 15, 35, 40,

45, 46, 53, 62, 71), Marion Pliner Collection (80), Constant E. Vaughn Collection (69), Ruth Yarbrough Collection (94); Virginia

Military Institute (86–91); Westbrook, *History of the 49th Pennsylvania Volunteers* (26).

The photographs appearing on pages 39, 76, and 96 were provided by the author.

When Johnny Went Marching

Library of Congress Cataloging-in-Publication Data

Wisler, G. Clifton.

When Johnny went marching : young Americans fight the Civil War / G. Clifton Wisler.

p.   cm.

Includes bibliographical references and index.

ISBN 0-688-16537-0 — ISBN 0-06-029242-3 (lib. bdg.)

1. United States—History—Civil War, 1861–1865—Participation, Juvenile—Juvenile literature. 2. United States—History—Civil War,
1861–1865—Children—Juvenile literature. 3. Child soldiers—United States—History—19th century—Juvenile literature. [1. United States—
History—Civil War, 1861–1865. 2. Child soldiers.] I. Title.

E585.C54 W57 2001   00-053617

973.7'0835—dc21   CIP

                                                                                                                                                    AC

Typography by Robbin Gourley and Jeanne Hogle

1 2 3 4 5 6 7 8 9 10

❖

First Edition

Contents

For my great-great-grandfathers who wore the blue

JOHN WESLEY HIGGINS, *13th Kansas Cavalry*

BERNARD MCCORMICK, *10th Illinois Cavalry*

NATHAN MILLER, *60th Ohio Infantry, 2nd Ohio Heavy Artillery*

REUBEN NELSON, *144th Indiana Infantry*

JOHN JACOB NEWCOMER, *1st Colorado Cavalry*

Introduction

Recently there has been a great revival of interest in the American Civil War (1861–65). No conflict in the history of the United States has been costlier in terms of human lives than this struggle between fellow countrymen. Of the four million soldiers and sailors who served actively on battlefields and at sea, more than six hundred thousand lost their lives. Thousands of others received disabling wounds, and countless numbers had their lives shortened by illness and disease.

It wasn't just the men in the ranks who experienced loss, though. No previous American war exposed civilians to suffering to such an extent. Women and girls played active roles as nurses and took their husbands', fathers', and brothers' places in field and factory. Several even undertook some of the most dangerous work of all—spying on their enemies. Females were not immune from bullets or germs. Young women also served in the ranks. Disguised as men and shielded from exposure by friends, husbands, or brothers, they were usually discovered only when they became sick or were wounded in action.

Although the presidents of the opposing sides, Abraham Lincoln and Jefferson

Davis, differed in many ways, they shared a common concern for their youngest citizens. As early as 1861, Lincoln forbade enlistment by soldiers under the age of eighteen without the written consent of their parents. A year later he prohibited their enlistment under any circumstances. Davis, in one of his earliest speeches, argued that taking young men under the age of eighteen into the ranks of battle was akin to the farmer who did not set aside part of his harvest as seed corn for the following year. Both leaders suffered the tragic loss of a son during the war.

Despite official prohibitions, and even after formal medical inspections of new recruits came to be required, boys as young as ten entered the ranks of both armies. Often the youngsters enlisted as musicians or orderlies. Some declined their pay and did not sign their regimental muster books. Even in the first days of the war, when recruiters were sometimes swamped with volunteers, many young men simply lied about their ages. Boys used names of older brothers or cousins. They occasionally traveled to areas where they were not well known. As the war continued, both armies needed to replace men killed in combat, taken prisoner, or dead from disease. Desperate recruiters learned to ignore the obvious youth of recruits.

For years Civil War historians have known about these boy soldiers and sailors. Bell Irvin Wiley, in his classic examination of the life of ordinary soldiers, *The Life of Billy Yank*, acknowledged the many young participants who served in the Northern army. His own survey of the official records of 14,330 soldiers from more than a hundred Union regiments revealed that close to one in fifty was under the age of eighteen at enlistment. Wiley also admitted that his number was low because it did not take into account soldiers who lied about their ages. In his companion volume, *The Life of Johnny Reb*, Wiley examined 11,000 Confederate infantry privates recruited in 1861 and 1862. One in twenty of these soldiers listed their age as seventeen or younger.[1]

In the pages that follow, I have attempted to put a face on these statistics. The reader will find wartime photographs of young men and women representing different regional, ethnic, and racial backgrounds. Some served briefly while others enlisted early and survived to see the end of hostilities. There are soldiers and spies, drummers and buglers, privates, one colonel, a future president, and six youngsters who were presented with our nation's highest military decoration, the Medal of Honor.

The uniforms, even in black and white, vary as much as the young people who wore them. Each had his or her personal reason for choosing one cause over another. Some found fame and future esteem while serving that cause, but many endured the same hardship and privation of their older comrades. Among the individuals depicted are many who paid the dearest price for their beliefs.

I must mention the many people who have contributed to this project. Michael Winey and Randy Hackenburg, curators of the United States Army Military History Institute's outstanding collection of photographs, made space for me in their limited facility on three separate visits. They enabled me to examine tens of thousands of photographs. The staff of the Illinois State Historical Library laid the foundations for this project when they introduced me to the John Logan Collection at Springfield in the spring of 1997. The many individuals who generously loaned precious photographs so that I could make copies, as well as the state and regional archives that assisted me in my work, are credited on page iv.

Finally I must thank Rosemary Brosnan, my longtime editor, who has been at my side from the genesis of this project all the way through to the end. One of my few regrets was the inability to discover a wartime photograph of Sergeant John Brosnan, Medal of Honor winner for gallantry at Petersburg and Rosemary's great-grandfather.

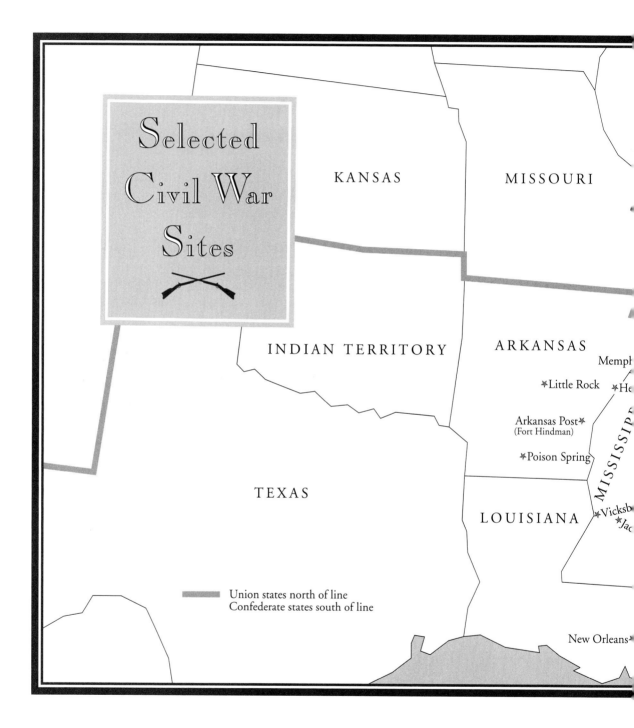

Selected Civil War Sites

KANSAS

MISSOURI

INDIAN TERRITORY

ARKANSAS

Memph

*Little Rock   *He

Arkansas Post*
(Fort Hindman)

*Poison Spring

MISSISSIPP

TEXAS

LOUISIANA   *Vicksb
*Jac

Union states north of line
Confederate states south of line

New Orleans*

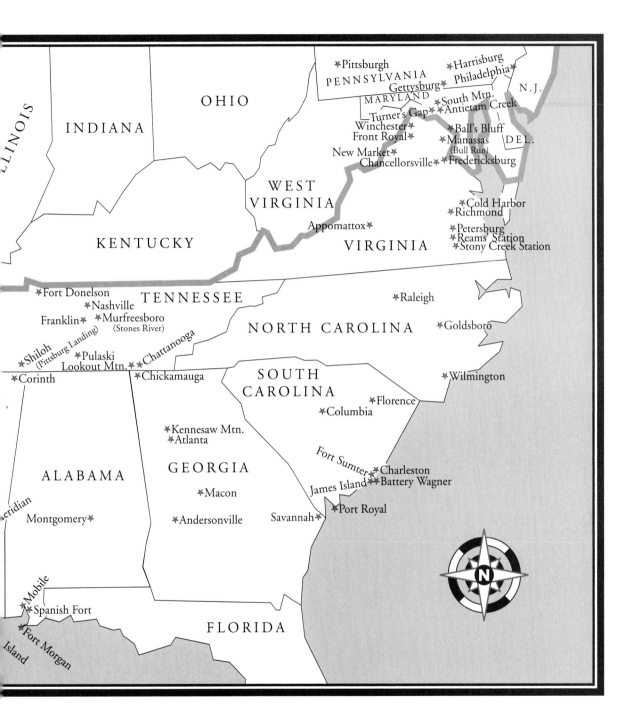

JOHN CLEM, *Michigan*

CHAPTER 1

The Runaways

Whether in the spirit of adventure, to avoid home and school responsibilities, or even to join a cherished father or brother in the ranks, many young soldiers ran away from home to join the army. Although each had his own reason, these runaway boys achieved fame far beyond what one would have expected of such pint-sized soldiers.

William Horsfall was the oldest son of Jonathan and Elizabeth Horsfall of Newport, Kentucky. Just thirteen years old when war broke out, he left home in December 1861 with three friends. They managed to sneak aboard a steamboat, but as the ship prepared to leave, William's young companions reconsidered and scampered home. William remained aboard. When discovered, he told the captain and passengers he was a poor orphan on his way to join the army. Playing the part for all it was worth, he was feasted and treated to a fine berth aboard the steamboat. He managed to join the Union Army's 1st Kentucky Infantry Regiment, then stationed in Ohio.[2]

On May 21, 1862, the 1st Kentucky Infantry was part of a Union army trying to drive the entrenched Confederates from the key rail center of Corinth, Mississippi. While probing for a weak point in the rebel lines, the regiment charged across a

WILLIAM HORSFALL, *Kentucky*

ravine. William, who was serving as Company G's drummer, set aside his drum and grabbed a rifle. Whether he was doing anything other than annoying the enemy is unknown, but an officer soon put an end to his amusements, ordering the boy to aid his wounded captain. The problem was that Captain Williamson, commanding the company, had been hit by a Confederate marksman during one of the recent charges. Wounded and trapped, the captain was in a desperate position.[3]

After leaning his gun against a tree, young Horsfall started forward in a stooping run. Dodging one way and then the other, he reached the captain and dragged him to where stretcher-bearers were waiting. In recognition of his daring feat, William Horsfall was awarded the Medal of Honor. He was not actually carried on the official muster roll of the regiment until a month later, following his fourteenth birthday.[4]

Born the same year as William Horsfall, Charles Bardeen had a different reason to join the army. From the time his father died when he was eleven years old, the boy had been "a disturbing element" to his mother. He had never been on good terms with his stepfather, and attempts to place him with friends and relatives had failed to bring about a change of attitude. Intelligent and fiercely opposed to slavery, the boy finally left home in July 1862. He made his way from Fitchburg, Massachusetts, to the state capital at Boston, where he joined the 1st Massachusetts Infantry.[5]

Although Bardeen enlisted as a drummer with Company D, he was reassigned as a fifer. Always quick to learn new things, he rapidly picked up the music. Once the fighting started, he pocketed his fife and undertook more perilous duty as a stretcher-bearer. When he wasn't comforting wounded comrades, he was forever annoying his elders with pranks or entertaining them with songs and stories.

Charles later remembered the day he discovered that his clothes were infested with lice:

> *The shirt was of thick wool with wide seams, and when I turned over the first seam I felt as if I should faint. There they were, big and little and nits, a garrison of them. I had had blue days since I enlisted, but this was the first time I wished I had staid home. Must I endure this sort of thing for three years?*[6]

He survived lice and worse during his army days. The self-confidence he developed in the camps and fields of eastern Virginia helped him in later life to become a scholar, educator, and publisher. His personal account of the war, *A Little Fifer's War Diary*, is one of the classic eyewitness accounts of the Civil War.

CHARLES BARDEEN, *Massachusetts*

Delavan Miller of Carthage, New York, also recorded his experiences during the war. He was still mourning his mother's death when war arrived. His father marched off with the 2nd New York Heavy Artillery, and Delavan felt like an orphan. Although only thirteen, he claimed to be eighteen years old in order to avoid asking his stepmother to sign enlistment papers. Recruiters took him into their

DELAVAN MILLER, *New York*

ranks as a drummer but warned that once they reached Washington, D.C., Del's father would likely send the boy home. The other soldiers argued Del's case, though, and Sergeant Loten Miller caved in. Del stayed.[7]

Del's closest call came in the trenches around Petersburg, Virginia, where his concern for his father's safety drew him perilously close to the action. Suddenly the Confederate batteries opened fire. "The air was full of hissing shells, which passed so close to us that we could feel their hot breath," Del was to write. Suddenly he felt something strike the side of his head. Convinced he had suffered a mortal wound, he clung to the ground and called for help. When his companions arrived, they found only a little bruise caused by a sliver of flying stone.[8]

Del's favorite memento of the war was a photograph of a ten-year-old Pennsylvania girl enclosed in a "soldier's companion," a small sewing kit. Knowing that someone was thinking of him and offering a small present lifted the cloud of despair brought on by the war's final winter of death and hardship.[9]

Perhaps no young soldier of the Civil War is better known than John Clem, "the Drummer Boy of Chickamauga." Only four feet tall when he left home to join the 22nd Michigan Infantry in September 1862, the blue-eyed, blond-haired eleven-year-old was as much a mascot as a drummer. That changed a year later when his regiment helped stem the Confederate attack at Chickamauga Creek in northern Georgia. In the heat of battle, he steadfastly beat his drum. Later he shouldered a musket.[10]

For most soldiers of any age, Johnny's actions at Chickamauga would have been enough. Johnny claimed that he had shot a rebel colonel, though. Later he added the title "Johnny Shiloh" despite the fact that he was still at home in Newark, Ohio, when that battle was fought. His regiment was not organized until sixth months later.[11]

It is not hard to imagine how a small boy, suddenly confronted with reporters, might exaggerate his importance. When his chance to stand up and help stiffen the defense came at Chickamauga, he did rise to the occasion. General George Thomas was so taken with the boy that he ordered Clem promoted to sergeant and assigned duties at army headquarters. Both sides needed heroes, and newspapers made one of the small Ohio boy with the king-size imagination. When Confederate cavalry captured the young sergeant in October, they used photographs of Clem to claim their enemy was sending babies to fight. Clem escaped his captors and returned to his regiment. Following the Confederate surrender, he stayed in the army. Eventually John Clem rose to the rank of major general. Today he rests at Arlington National Cemetery.[12]

ISABELLA "BELLE" BOYD, *West Virginia*

CHAPTER 2

Stonewall's Spy

Isabella "Belle" Boyd was born in 1844 in Berkeley County in what is now West Virginia. She grew up in and around the town of Martinsburg and had recently graduated from Mount Washington College in Baltimore, Maryland, when war broke out. In the Shenandoah Valley, residents and even families often found themselves on opposite sides. Martinsburg was occupied by United States Army forces early in the war. When federal soldiers broke into her father's store on Independence Day, 1861, seventeen-year-old Belle reportedly chased them away with gunfire. Afterward she befriended many of the lonely young Union officers in order to gain valuable information on federal operations. She then sent notes to Confederate General Thomas J. "Stonewall" Jackson and advised him of the enemy plans.[13]

After one of her messages was intercepted, Belle was summoned to army headquarters and warned that she might be considered a spy if she continued. She left Martinsburg and spent several months as a nurse and courier. Then, in the spring of 1862, she was captured by Union cavalry and taken to Baltimore. Her brief imprisonment came to an end when her captors failed to produce proof that she was a spy. Once freed, she resumed her illegal activities.[14]

On May 23, 1862, she was surprised to find the Union soldiers in Martinsburg frantically running around. When she asked one of her young soldier acquaintances what was happening, he informed her that Confederates were marching toward the town. More importantly, he explained that Union soldiers were preparing to burn a huge Union supply depot at Front Royal, Virginia, to prevent its capture by Confederates. Belle immediately set off to inform her friends of the need to hurry.[15]

Racing between lines of Union and Confederate riflemen, dodging exploding shells, Belle finally spotted a column of approaching rebel horsemen.

As I neared our line I waved my bonnet to our soldiers, to intimate that they should press forward, upon which one regiment, the First Maryland "rebel" Infantry, and Hay's Louisiana Brigade, gave me a loud cheer, and, without waiting for further orders, dashed upon the town at a rapid pace.[16]

While her activities made her a Confederate celebrity, they also earned her more and more attention from her enemies. She was arrested again in July 1862 and confined in the Old Capital Prison in Washington, D.C. A month later she was released in an exchange of prisoners. When she was captured again the following summer, Belle spent half a year in prison. Upon her release this time, she was warned not to return to Union-held territory unless she wished to face a hangman.[17]

After a short time in Richmond, Virginia, she set sail for England carrying Confederate dispatches. Unfortunately her ship was captured. The young Union officer placed in charge, Samuel Hardinge Jr., soon fell under Belle's enchanting spell. Whether with his help or perhaps because he was distracted, she managed to escape to Canada. From there Belle sailed aboard a British ship to England. In

August 1864, she wed her former captor there. Their marriage was a short one. When Hardinge returned to the United States, he was arrested and charged with treason. Belle, who had remained in London, was in dire need of money. She supported herself by writing her memoirs, *Belle Boyd in Camp and Prison*. She also embarked on a new career, portraying herself on stage. Meanwhile her book, published in 1865 in London and New York, assured her status as a celebrity. When word came that Hardinge had died in the reunited United States in 1866, Belle devoted all her energies to the theater.[18]

Before large crowds and to thunderous applause, she reenacted her most daring exploits. Upon returning to the United States, she was surprised to find willing audiences for her performances there as well. After many of the more famous characters in her wartime drama were long dead, Belle continued to spin her romantic tales of the girl spy who had outfoxed one pursuer after another. Her adoring public was shocked when she suddenly fell victim to a heart attack at Kilbourne City, Wisconsin, in 1900. Ironically, the most famous Southern spy was buried in one of the northernmost states of the country.[19]

CHAPTER 3

The Youngest Hero

Willie Johnston never expected to be called a hero. In fact, he didn't imagine himself a soldier. As young friends from his hometown of St. Johnsbury, Vermont, flocked to the nearby fair grounds to sign up with the 3rd Vermont Infantry, Willie was busy sewing buttons on uniforms at his father's tailor shop. By December 1861, things had changed. The Vermont boys suffered severe losses at the first battle of Bull Run, and recruiters were having a difficult time finding volunteers. Willie's father saw the boom in business die, too. In need of money, he signed on as a substitute, a soldier paid a bounty by a town in order to free others from military service. Willie, who had been serving as a volunteer drummer for regimental recruiters, saw his chance. With his older brother James at home to look after their mother, Willie enlisted in his father's regiment and left for Washington, D.C.[20]

Willie was not yet twelve when, as drummer for Company D of the 3rd Vermont Infantry, he saw his first action during the Peninsula campaign of 1862. With a hundred thousand federal troops within sight of Richmond, Confederate commander Joseph E. Johnston launched a desperate attack. General Johnston himself was wounded, and for a brief time it appeared that Richmond would fall and the war might be over. Confederate President Jefferson Davis turned to his military aide, General Robert E. Lee, and sent him out to take charge. In a series of frantic battles known as the Seven Days, Lee's outnumbered rebels drove the federal army from Richmond.[21]

With their backs to a river and thousands of Confederates marching relentlessly toward them, the Union army formed itself on the slopes of Malvern Hill. Backed by hundreds of cannons, they stood their ground and waited. Rebel regiments launched a final, desperate attack, hoping to destroy their enemy that hot July afternoon. Instead, hundreds of gray-clad soldiers fell in heaps. The Union line held.

Willie saw it all. Dazed and a bit bedraggled, he had lost most of his gear in the mad retreat. His clothes were torn and ragged. But through it all he held on to his drum, for he realized that without it, he was useless to his friends and comrades. When the Vermont Brigade assembled for a grand review that next week, Willie was surprised to see President Abraham Lincoln there. The youngster was also startled to discover that he alone of all the drummers in the brigade had managed to bring away his drum. With a few fifers, Willie formed a makeshift band to play for the visitors. President Lincoln, surprised to see a lone drummer, paused to share a few words with the boy. Willie, embarrassed and shy, did his best to explain that he had done nothing special. At scarcely five feet tall, Willie was dwarfed by the much taller Lincoln. Before leaving, the president asked the young drummer's name.[22]

"It's Willie, sir," the boy answered. Lincoln, whose own son Willie had recently died of a fever, grew faint. With the help of several officers, the president made it to the shade of a nearby tree and sat down to rest.

It was not to be their final meeting. Willie became sick that summer and was

WILLIE JOHNSTON, *Vermont*

confined at Chesapeake General Hospital near Fort Monroe, Virginia. When he failed to recover, doctors sent him to Baltimore. Once Willy was well, he discovered that the army had decided to assign its underage soldiers to duty tending wounded comrades. Willie remained in Baltimore as a nurse and orderly.[23]

He was still there in September 1863 when an officer appeared and ordered him to Washington, D.C. Willie must have felt confused. Soldiers led him to a large wooden bathtub and scrubbed him from head to toe. A barber clipped his hair and gave him what Willie remembered as an unneeded shave. Finally, dressed in a fine new silk uniform, Willie Johnston boarded a train for the short trip to Washington. In the reception hall of the War Department, with generals and congressmen looking on, Drummer Johnston, then just thirteen years old, found himself facing Colonel E. D. Townsend, assistant adjutant general of the entire United States Army. After speaking a few words to the crowd, the colonel presented Willie Johnston the Medal of Honor.[24]

Lincoln had not forgotten the ragged boy who shared his son's name. After the ceremony, the president visited privately with the youngest soldier ever to receive his country's highest military decoration. There is no record of what was said, but the great man left with a livelier step and a young boy stood a little taller. The accompanying photograph, taken the day of the ceremony, shows Willie wearing his medal. The following day he set aside his new uniform and resumed his duties. Before the war was over, he was back with the 3rd Vermont Infantry.[25]

In 1866 Willie enrolled at Norwich University at Northfield, Vermont, where he performed in the cadet band. After four years of study, he graduated with the class of 1870. Although the rest of his life remains a mystery, he is reported to have lived until 1936.[26]

CHAPTER 4

The Heartbeat of the Army

Perhaps the most enduring of all Civil War images is the picture of the young drummer, marching alongside his older brothers or father, encouraging his comrades to greater efforts. Edwin Forbes, artist and wartime correspondent, offered the following description:

Ah! Well, the soldiers would have missed other comrades far less than the lively little drummers, and many marches through scorching sun and suffocating dust would have been much harder to bear had it not been for these little musicians. Lagging foot-steps often quickened and weary faces brightened at the sudden sound of drum and fife, and many a "God bless you, boys; you give us cheer" went out to them in the long march.[27]

The Civil War drummer had a far more important role to play than that of inspiring his comrades, though. In a time before radios, when a single officer needed to command hundreds of men, the drum became his voice. The drummer who sounded a timely alarm might save his company or regiment from a surprise onslaught. He sounded calls announcing mealtime, drill, assembly, and bedtime. Unlike drummers in previous wars, he often set aside his drum when battle lines were formed, tied a white kerchief around his arm, and became stretcher-bearer and medic. He performed daring rescues and consoled the dying.

Typical of the boys who rushed into Confederate service was thirteen-year-old Charles E. Mosby. Just a schoolboy and the only son of Sarah Mosby of Henrico County, Virginia, Charles joined Company I of the 6th Virginia Infantry in June 1861. His regiment served along the Atlantic coast of North Carolina in February 1862 before retreating to Norfolk, Virginia. Worn down by hard

CHARLES E. MOSBY, *Virginia*

marches and fierce winter weather, Charles returned to his home near Richmond. The boy was clearly too ill to return to action, and his mother pleaded for his discharge. Confederate authorities agreed, and he was excused from service as underage and unfit for service. Nevertheless, when federal armies threatened his home, he returned to service, joining Henderson's 19th Virginia Heavy Artillery Battery in November 1862 and serving actively throughout the remainder of the war.[28]

Myron Philo Walker was a remarkable young man. He began drumming as a twelve-year-old schoolboy in Belchertown, Massachusetts. He often practiced with his older brother Frank, who belonged to a town band. In the spring of 1861, when war broke out, Myron was graduating from the local high school. Determined to join the Union army, he made his way to nearby Springfield to enlist in the 10th Massachusetts Infantry. After demonstrating his ability to drum and march, Myron was disappointed to learn he didn't measure up. Captain Joseph Parsons of Company C explained that because he was only four feet four inches tall, Myron was unable to take the twenty-eight-inch step required by the army. In addition, being just fourteen, he would need his parents' permission.[29]

MYRON PHILO WALKER,
Massachusetts

Myron reappeared the following day with his mother, who signed his enlistment papers. He hadn't grown any taller, but the officers of Company D were in desperate need of soldiers and accepted him anyway. In January 1862, a month short of his fifteenth birthday, he was wounded by the accidental discharge of a pistol and sent home. By September he was back in the army, though. He quickly became the pet of the regiment. His fellow soldiers often found him extra food, and officers let him ride their horses on long marches.[30]

The 10th Massachusetts Infantry was part of the Union's Army of the Potomac. Myron witnessed bitter fighting throughout Virginia and helped turn back Confederate General Robert E. Lee's invading armies at Antietam Creek in

Maryland in 1862 and at Gettysburg, Pennsylvania, in 1863. Along with his fellow musicians, Myron tended wounded comrades and provided what comfort he could to the dying. On November 9, 1862, though, it was Myron who required sympathy. That was the day the plucky drummer learned his father had died at home in Massachusetts. Many in Company D recalled that day as one of their darkest.[31]

After the war Myron had a long and distinguished career in business and politics. A wealthy insurance executive, he personally hosted a grand regimental reunion of the 10th Massachusetts Infantry in 1881. The ten thousand guests included the state governor and most of the legislature. He won election to the state senate in 1884 and lost a close election to the U. S. House of Representatives in 1888. That same year Union veterans elected him to the esteemed post of commander of the Massachusetts Department of the Grand Army of the Republic. At the forty-second reunion of

THOMAS PENNYPACKER, *New Jersey*

the 10th Massachusetts Association in 1910, the hundred surviving soldiers honored their former drummer. Myron died on March 25 the following year.[32]

Thomas Pennypacker was another veteran of the Army of the Potomac. Thomas lied about his age when he signed up as drummer for Company H of the 3rd New Jersey Infantry in August 1862. At four feet six inches tall, he must not have been a very convincing sixteen-year-old. He needed his father's signature on his enlistment papers. A resident of Woodbury, Tom was not the best musician. He was excused duty to learn music the following spring. Once he completed his lessons, he proved an able soldier.[33]

The 3rd New Jersey had a number of hard fights. One of the most dramatic moments came on May 3, 1863, during the battle of Chancellorsville in Virginia. After advancing three miles, it met with a murderous fire from the Confederate line. For two and a half hours, the regiment held its ground. Thomas devoted those hours to offering water to his weary comrades and helping the wounded find shelter and medical aid. Finally, with their ammunition nearly exhausted and with ninety-nine of their number killed, wounded, or missing, they gave way.[34]

When his enlistment expired in June 1864, Thomas transferred to the 15th New Jersey Infantry. He was with those veteran fighters when they defended the nation's capital from Confederate General Jubal Early's army in July 1864. The 15th New Jersey then drove Early from Virginia's vital Shenandoah Valley and participated in the dramatic Union victory at Petersburg in April 1865. After witnessing the surrender of Robert E. Lee's Army of Northern Virginia on April 9, 1865, Thomas was discharged from the army in June.[35]

Drummer David Martin of Linn County, Iowa, performed his wartime service with the illustrious 31st Iowa Infantry. Just fourteen when the war began, he and his two brothers worked at nearby farms after school in order to support their widowed mother. David remained at home until August 15, 1862, when he stretched himself to his full five foot one inch height and enlisted at Cedar Rapids. The fair-haired, blue-eyed youngster served ably as Company A's drummer. Except for an unexplained absence that first August, David was present at every muster until his regiment was finally discharged by a grateful nation on June 27, 1865.[36]

In almost three years of active duty, David participated in some of the most decisive fighting of the war. The 31st Iowa Infantry was involved in heavy fighting during the siege of Vicksburg, Mississippi. Later the regiment marched with General William T. Sherman from Chattanooga, Tennessee, to Atlanta, Georgia, and made the destructive march from the ashes of that city to the Georgia port of Savannah. After "Shermanizing" the Carolinas, capturing both Charleston and Columbia, David Martin witnessed the surrender of Confederate General Joseph E. Johnston's army outside Goldsboro, North Carolina.

DAVID MARTIN, *Iowa*

Perhaps the regiment's hottest fight was the capture of Lookout Mountain near Chattanooga, Tennessee. Andrew Henderson, of Company F, described it as follows:

The firing now became terrific, in many places the opposing forces were not ten feet apart, separated only by some rocks or sheltered by trees. Along both lines a continuous and deafening fire of musketry was kept up until 12 o'clock at night.[37]

Like many youngsters who set off to find the great adventure of their lives in the army, David Martin must have welcomed the chance to return home.

CHAPTER 5

A Reckless Charge

One young Confederate driving the Union forces from Richmond in 1862 was Edwin Francis Jemison of New Orleans, Louisiana. The Louisiana Tigers, as they were known, fought with a desperation fueled by a desire for revenge. That spring New Orleans had fallen into federal hands, and the soldiers feared for the fate of their families. Rumors of outrages committed by Union General Benjamin Butler's troops had reached Virginia. In the accompanying photograph, Francis Jemison's eyes reflect the anxiety of a young man facing his first great battle while worrying about his mother and younger brothers and sisters at home. Probably just fourteen years old on that fateful July 1, 1862, he had exaggerated his age in order to enlist with the 2nd Louisiana Infantry Regiment. Now, heeding the call of their commanders to "Remember Butler and the women of New Orleans," he charged into the teeth of Yankee rifle and cannon fire at Malvern Hill.[38]

It took the Louisianans five minutes to cover the last three hundred yards. All the while friends were falling to the right and left. The few who managed to reach the summit engaged briefly in hand-to-hand combat. Then they simply melted away. The whole charge had taken less than half an hour. The 2nd Louisiana had 182 men killed or wounded that day, including its commanding colonel and major. Among the mortally wounded was Francis Jemison, who died before the sun set.[39]

EDWIN FRANCIS JEMISON, *Louisiana*

CHAPTER 6

A Brother's Sacrifice

Patton John and his brother Reason had always been close. As the second and third sons in a large family, they helped each other with school lessons and joined their older brother, Cephas, working on neighboring farms to earn a few extra dollars. Seven months after the outbreak of the Civil War, eighteen-year-old Patton joined the 32nd Illinois Infantry. The regiment served ably under General Ulysses S. Grant at Forts Henry and Donelson before moving up the Tennessee River to Pittsburg Landing. A small Methodist meetinghouse, Shiloh Church, stood nearby.[40]

In the early hours of April 6, 1862, Confederate General Albert Sidney Johnston's army surprised the scattered Union forces and drove toward the landing. Johnston hoped to cut off the federal army from its base and force it to surrender. The 32nd Illinois Infantry occupied a critical position along the only decent road to the landing. As one regiment after another was driven back, a single thin line of privates bought time for the rest of the army to form a new defense line. One by one those brave men's rifles fell silent. The Confederates swarmed out of the woods and encircled thousands of defiant Yankees in what came to be known as the Hornet's Nest.[41]

One of the fallen heroes that day at the battle of Shiloh was Patton John. History might be excused for overlooking the action of a single man on a day when his regiment alone suffered 158 casualties. Reason never forgot his beloved brother, though, and when his chance came, he joined the Union army and finished what his brother had begun. In remembering the brother who had so often set an example, Reason recalled a few lines written by Scottish poet Robert Burns:

> The pitying heart that felt for human woe,
> The dauntless heart that feared no human pride,
> The friend of man, to vice alone a foe,
> For ev'n his failings lean'd to virtue's side.[42]

PATTON JOHN, *Illinois*

Chapter 7

The Bloodiest Day

In the autumn of 1862, it must have seemed to many Americans that the South was destined to win its independence. Confederate General Braxton Bragg was leading an army through Kentucky, threatening to bring war to the midwestern states. In the East, rebels under General Robert E. Lee had driven the Union Army of the Potomac from the gates of Richmond, smashed another federal army commanded by John Pope at the old battlefield of Bull Run at Manassas, Virginia, and were across the Potomac River in Maryland, threatening Washington, Baltimore, and perhaps even Philadelphia. Both Southern armies expected warm welcomes and scores of recruits. Instead Bragg fought an inconclusive battle at Perryville, Kentucky, and returned to Tennessee. Lee fought his way through the mountains of western Maryland but found his path blocked on September 17 at the small town of Sharpsburg, Maryland. In the bloody battle that followed, named by Union commander George McClellan for Antietam Creek, more men died in a single day than at any other time in the war.

Fourteen-year-old John Cook left his mother, brothers, and sisters in Cincinnati, Ohio, in order to sign on as bugler with Battery B of the 4th U. S. Artillery. The ferocious fighting at Antietam left his unit in desperate shape. Their commander, Captain Joseph Campbell, was hit early, and John was assigned to assist him to safer ground. Rather than remain with the captain, John raced back and arrived to find his battery involved in a terrific duel with Confederate guns and riflemen. Although he was the battery bugler, John went to work, serving first as a cannoneer and later as a gunner. Lieutenant James Stewart, recommending John Cook for a Medal of Honor, wrote, "his courage and conduct in that battle was the admiration of all who witnessed it." Today a memorial tablet marks the spot on the Antietam battlefield where the bugler helped stem a rebel counterattack and preserve the Union.[43]

The 49th Pennsylvania Infantry was one of the units urgently dispatched to help block the rebel invaders' path. Charley King of West Chester, Pennsylvania, had joined as Company F's drummer a year and eight days before. Young Charley had lied

JOHN COOK, *Ohio*

about his age, but he left home with his father's blessing. Believers in the Union cause, both father and son felt the need to support the army. Charley couldn't mask his small size and twelve-year-old appearance. But his good-natured smile soon won the hearts of his comrades. When his father had misgivings about putting his oldest son in danger, the soldiers vowed to look after their young drummer.[44]

It wasn't always easy to persuade Charley to stay to the rear. The previous summer, during the advance on Richmond and the Seven Days battles, the 49th had seen its share of hard fighting. By the time the regiment reached the Antietam battlefield, they were weary. For once Charley agreed to stay in the rear with the other drummers and tend the wounded. It was about that time that their brigade commander, General Winfield Scott Hancock, rode up. "Boys, do as you have done before; be brave and true, and I think this will be your last battle," Hancock told the Pennsylvanians.[45]

The words were to prove prophetic, although not in the way intended. The 49th

CHARLES KING, *Pennsylvania*

Pennsylvania remained in reserve most of the day, suffering only a few casualties from Confederate sharpshooters and artillery. Unfortunately for Charley, one rebel shell overshot the front line and struck him in the body. The boy collapsed in a heap. Charley was in great pain from his wound, but he endured it bravely. His thoughts were of home and family. After lingering three days, the thirteen-year-old died on September 20, the youngest of the thousands killed on that bloodiest day of the war. His father, who had hurried to the battlefield after receiving news of Charley's wound, had the sad duty of bringing his son's shattered body home to West Chester for burial. Charley's entire regiment went into mourning.[46]

CHAPTER 8

"A Perfect Rain of Bullets"

For many young Southerners, the Civil War represented an attack on their homes and families. John Baird and his sister June lived in a Jacksonport, Arkansas, boardinghouse before South Carolina militia opened fire on the Union garrison occupying Fort Sumter at Charleston, South Carolina. For a time it appeared that Arkansas might stay out of the Confederacy. When secession was announced, the call went out for volunteers to defend the state. John was probably just fifteen when he posed for the picture on page 28 with his nineteen-year-old neighbor Henry Clements. The two boys had just entered the ranks of the Jackson Guards, who became Company G, 1st Arkansas Infantry. Ahead lay almost four years of bloody fighting.[47]

John claimed to be eighteen in order to join, and with dizzying rapidity he found himself riding railroad cars across the entire Confederacy. Two weeks after leaving home, he was in Virginia. Following the first battle of Bull Run, the Arkansans were sent back west. On April 6–7, 1862, they won distinction at the battle of Shiloh in southern Tennessee.[48]

JOHN BAIRD AND HENRY CLEMENTS, *Arkansas*

Colonel James F. Fagan, the regiment's commanding officer, reported:

We engaged the enemy three different times, and braved a perfect rain of bullets, shot and shell. Exposed, facing great odds, with the enemy in front and on the flank, the regiment endured a murderous fire until endurance ceased to be a virtue. Three different times did we go into that valley of death, and as often were forced back by overwhelming numbers intrenched in a strong position.[49]

Shortly thereafter John won promotion to corporal. The effects of war, the loss of friends, and the loneliness took their toll, though. In July 1863, during the hard fighting around Atlanta, he was wounded. John returned to duty but was never again entirely healthy. On March 25, 1865, he entered a Macon, Georgia, hospital. He was still there in April when Union cavalry arrived and accepted his surrender.[50]

Henry Elms was the eldest son of David and Malinda Elms of Honey Creek, Texas. They grew corn and raised cattle and horses on their 160-acre farm. When he enlisted November 3, 1861, in the 6th Texas Infantry, Henry listed his age at eighteen, but he was actually six months younger. If he was expecting glory and excitement under the Confederate banner, he soon found himself disappointed.[51]

The 6th Texas Infantry was stationed at Fort Hindman at Arkansas Post. The fort guarded the Arkansas River approach to the state capital at Little Rock. In January 1863, a large Union army surrounded the fort. Hopelessly outnumbered, battered by artillery and gunboats, the garrison was forced to surrender. Henry found himself at the mercy of his enemies.[52]

Loaded aboard steamboats, they faced a new ordeal.

The scantily clothed prisoners suffered terribly from the cold weather. William J. Oliphant wrote that their "faces were struck by the thickly falling snow . . . as though

HENRY ELMS, *Texas*

smitten by driving particles of glass, and the icy wind chilled us to the marrow." He added, "Many of the prisoners afterward lost limbs from being frostbitten, and scarce a day passed that we did not leave a lonely grave by the side of the great 'Father of Waters.'"[53]

The men of the 6th Texas Infantry who survived their journey were loaded aboard boxcars and taken to Camp Butler, a prison camp near Springfield, Illinois. That February more than a hundred prisoners died of disease at Camp Butler. The only remedy seemed to be taking an oath of allegiance to the United States. Many men took the oath and were released. Henry refused. In April he and the other survivors of his regiment boarded a train, were taken to Virginia, and were exchanged for captured Union prisoners.[54]

Henry returned to action during the summer of 1863. His regiment fought hard at Chickamauga and suffered heavy losses at Franklin and Nashville during General John Bell Hood's Tennessee campaign in 1864. Afterward they joined General Joseph E. Johnston's army in North Carolina. Following General Robert E. Lee's surrender at Appomattox Courthouse, Johnston surrendered in late April 1865.[55]

After the war Henry returned to Texas. He married in July 1868 and settled with his wife in Jackson County, Oklahoma. They prospered there, raising five children. On September 5, 1912, Henry died and was buried in Frances Cemetery.[56]

CHAPTER 9

Two Brothers

Boys frequently enlisted in regiments to join fathers or elder brothers, but at least one Illinois boy joined his *younger* brother's regiment. Orion Howe, who was to win a Medal of Honor for gallantry outside Vicksburg, Mississippi, was a relative latecomer to the war. His younger brother Lyston signed up with the 15th Illinois Infantry when he was still three months short of his eleventh birthday. The two Howe boys had always been close. Their mother's death when both were little had brought sadness and heartache. A stepmother provided only misery. Both Howes were accomplished drummers. Their father, a veteran musician who fought in the war with Mexico, taught them to beat drums as small children. While this caused some annoyance to neighbors, it prepared the boys for their wartime service.

Lyston may well have been the youngest soldier to have seen action from 1861 to 1865. When the boys' father, William Howe, accepted a post with the 15th Infantry, Lyston signed on as well. The Howes served ably during the early campaigns in Missouri. Cold, damp weather soon took a toll on Lyston, though. Barely over four feet tall, he began running a dangerously high fever. Army surgeons, believing him near death, discharged the eleven-year-old in October 1861 and sent him to his grandmother in Chicago.[57]

Lyston surprised everyone by regaining his health. With Orion and their grandmother's constant tending, he quickly recovered. Soon the Howes were drumming for the newly formed 55th Illinois Infantry. When in February 1862 their father was transferred to that regiment as fife major, the principal musician and conductor of the regimental band, both boys wanted to enlist, too. Again Lyston was allowed to go. Orion remained in Chicago attending school. While William and Lyston Howe survived two days of bitter fighting at Shiloh that April, Orion fumed and plotted. Eventually he escaped his grandmother's watchful eye, sneaked aboard a southbound train, hid on a Mississippi supply boat, and talked his way onto a supply wagon bound for Memphis, Tennessee. Once there, he located the camp of the 55th Infantry and persuaded Lieutenant Colonel Oscar Malmborg to allow him to become drummer for Company C.[58]

LYSTON D. HOWE, *Illinois*

If Lyston proved to be a spirited and dependable soldier, Orion soon became the pet of the entire outfit. From his enlistment in September 1862 at age thirteen, he was continually amusing his companions, outwitting officers, and dreaming up mischievous schemes for his brother and the regiment's other drummers. In February 1863, when their father left the army, the two youngsters again found themselves on their own.[59]

Perhaps it was the months spent living and fighting and suffering with the men of Company C that led Orion Howe to perform one of the most daring and reckless deeds of the Vicksburg campaign. On May 19 Union General William T. Sherman directed an assault on the fortified Confederate lines shielding Vicksburg from attack by land forces. The 55th Illinois managed to make its way up the appropriately named Graveyard Road to within a few hundred yards of the enemy before concentrated rifle and cannon fire trapped them in a narrow ravine. With men falling every minute, Orion found it difficult to remain at his post in the rear. Soon he was offering water to the wounded. As ammunition became short, he rushed out among the wounded and dying to retrieve their cartridge boxes. Colonel Malmborg, fearing for the young man's safety, sent him instead back to the main body of the army with a request for the needed ammunition.[60]

Orion took off like a shot across the battlefield, dodging bullets as his companions went down one by one. He was halfway to safety when a Confederate musket ball tore through the fleshy part of his right thigh. When the boy got to his feet and limped on, sighs of relief could be heard all along the federal line. Upon reaching the main Union line, Orion, despite pain and loss of blood, made his way to General Sherman and described the terrible plight of his regiment. Sherman ordered help and commanded Orion be sent to a hospital.[61]

Impressed with the boy, the general arranged his admission to the U. S. Naval Academy, temporarily relocated to Newport, Rhode Island. Orion's entry was delayed because while running dispatches near Dallas, Georgia, he picked up a discarded rifle and fired toward a group of lounging Confederates. Orion was a better drummer than sharpshooter, and he missed. The rebels, angered at the interruption of their peaceful afternoon, returned fire, striking Orion twice in the arm and once in the chest. He spent several months recovering from his wounds, but in 1865 the boy soldier became a midshipman. Unfortunately Orion had trouble accepting the strict discipline required of future naval officers. He accumulated demerits for "skylarking at seamanship" and "throwing bread at mess." Following the close of his second year, he was dismissed.[62]

Orion's adventures were not yet over, though. He served with the merchant marine until shipwrecked off the coast of Ireland. He accompanied the army as a civilian scout during its campaign against the Modoc Indians. During the battle of the Lava Beds in northern California, he was wounded and left for dead. A Modoc whom Orion had befriended carried him back to the army camp so that he could recover. Later, during President Grover Cleveland's administration, veteran Union regiments were afforded the opportunity to nominate one of their own as a candidate for the Medal of Honor. The 55th Illinois chose Orion Howe, and on April 23, 1896, he received the belated reward for heroism. In 1888, at a unit reunion, Orion was asked about his exploits. He replied that the efforts of his comrades to give notoriety to his deeds "were most often embarrassing." He insisted he never did anything beyond what was expected of a soldier doing his duty. Few present agreed.[63]

COL. OSCAR MALMBORG AND ORION HOWE, *Illinois*

RICHARD KIRKLAND, *South Carolina*

CHAPTER 10

The Angel of Marye's Heights

Following the bloody fighting at Antietam, the Union Army of the Potomac got a new commander. Ambrose Burnside had distinguished himself in numerous battles, but privately he was unsure of his ability to command an army. In December 1862, he confronted the Confederate forces of Robert E. Lee in entrenched positions at Fredericksburg, Virginia. In massive frontal assaults, federal troops charged the enemy. Nowhere was the fighting more intense than at a stone wall below Marye's Heights, a low ridge overlooking the town. Lee's men cut the attacking federals to ribbons, leaving thousands dead and dying. It was little more than hopeless slaughter. Afterward, Lee remarked, "It is well that war is so terrible—we should grow too fond of it."[64]

As darkness settled over the snow-covered slopes, wounded soldiers cried out for aid and water. One Confederate sergeant, nineteen-year-old Richard Kirkland of the 2nd South Carolina Infantry, could not stand idly by. He begged his captain and then his colonel for permission to offer what help he could to the wounded enemy.

Both refused. Finally, he approached his friend and neighbor General J. B. Kershaw.[65]

"Kirkland, don't you know that you could get a bullet through your head the moment you stepped over the wall?" the general asked.[66]

Richard acknowledged the danger, but even when the general refused to allow the young sergeant permission to display a white kerchief, insisted on trying. Armed only with canteens provided by his fellow soldiers, he crossed the wall and made his way among the wounded enemy, offering the comfort of a drink, whispering a prayer, or tightening a bandage. Down the hill, wary of Confederate attack, Union marksmen witnessed the shadowy figure. Soon word of the kindhearted rebel's actions trickled down the line, though, and instead of firing, the bluecoats cheered. For an hour and a half the young South Carolinian made his rounds, pausing only to refill his canteens. One time firing resumed, only to stop when Kirkland reappeared. Shamed by the selfless act of a solitary soldier, the generals arranged a truce, and the following day surgeons attended the wounded and carried them from the field.[67]

Richard Kirkland continued his Civil War service, winning promotion to lieutenant at Gettysburg. Then, on September 19, 1863, while leading a charge at the battle of Chickamauga in northern Georgia, he was shot in the chest. Although anguished comrades tried to carry him to safety, he refused. "I am done for," he told them. "You can do me no good. Save yourselves and tell my pa I died right."[68]

Richard Kirkland died a month after celebrating his twentieth birthday. He was far from forgotten, though. In 1909 his body was reburied at the Quaker Cemetery in Camden near the grave of his commander, J. B. Kershaw. A memorial fountain was erected in his honor. At Prince of Peace Episcopal Church in Gettysburg, grateful former enemies placed a memorial tablet to "a hero of benevolence." Today, at the

Richard Kirkland Monument, Fredericksburg National Military Park

base of Marye's Heights, a monument depicts a compassionate South Carolina sergeant offering a wounded enemy a drink of water. It is perhaps the most visited spot on the battlefield.[69]

PATRICK CORR *(Ireland), Massachusetts*

CHAPTER 11

The Immigrants

Some of the staunchest supporters of the Union cause were idealistic European-born citizens, eager to prove their worth to their adopted nation. Although immigrants also served in the Confederate army, more joined the Union cause. While the Union blockade closed Southern ports, ships carrying Irish and German families to New York and Boston were often greeted by recruiting bands and officers eager to enlist the newcomers to fill the thinning files of their regiments.

Foreign-born soldiers who had already settled in the United States also flocked to recruiting stations. Many saw opportunity for useful employment in the army while others hoped to escape the drudgery of life at home. Patrick Corr was one example. Born in County Cavan, Ireland, Patrick arrived in Massachusetts as an eleven-year-old. Eight years later he was living in Lowell, Massachusetts. Although he could neither read nor write, he managed to eke out a living before enlisting with the 30th Massachusetts Infantry on November 25, 1861. As a corporal in Company I, Patrick participated in the capture of Ship Island off the Gulf Coast of Mississippi and was with Benjamin Butler's triumphant army when it took possession of New

Orleans, Louisiana, the South's largest city.[70]

In the summer of 1864 his regiment moved to Virginia's Shenandoah Valley. Patrick soon found himself in trouble. He was arrested and tried before a military court. Found guilty, he was sentenced

to be confined at hard labor at Dry Tortugas, Florida, for the period of six years— to wear during the first two years a ball weighing twenty-four (24) lbs. attached to his left leg by a chain six feet in length, and to forfeit to the United States all pay and allowances of bounty now due or that may become due him from the United States.

Patrick must have shuddered to hear the pronouncement of such a harsh sentence. His regimental officers were also concerned. Near Port Hudson, Louisiana, in 1863, Patrick was struck by a shell fragment. He still limped from a second injury. In consideration of his earlier good service, the sentence was reduced to confinement at New York for the balance of his enlistment. Patrick was released in April 1866. From that time until his death on October 22, 1908, he proved himself a worthy citizen of his adopted land.[71]

The 30th Massachusetts was one of many Civil War units to wear the colorful French Zouave uniform. The fancy caps proved unsuitable in the sultry South, and the baggy trousers quickly became rags when traveling the briar-choked countryside. Most Zouave regiments adopted standard Union dress after their first months of service. On page 40 Patrick Corr appears in a photograph taken in the war's early months.

Another Irish-born teenager to serve the Union cause was Thomas C. Murphy. Red-haired Tom enlisted on September 18, 1861, in the 31st Illinois Infantry.

Although he listed his age as eighteen, he was actually two years younger. The eldest of five children, he saw the army as a way off the farm and a chance to make a name for himself. He accomplished both. By March 1862 he had won his corporal's stripes.[72]

Then, on May 22, 1863, during the second attack on the Confederate fortifications at Vicksburg, Mississippi, he braved a blistering fire from rebel cannons and rifles and managed for a short time to mount the parapet of a Confederate fort before being wounded. Carried from the field, he spent the following four months recovering his strength. To his dismay, he returned to his regiment to find he had been reduced to his old rank of private. Discouraged and never completely healthy again,

he left the army when his enlistment expired in September 1864. Thirty years after his gallant charge at Vicksburg, he was awarded the Medal of Honor "for conspicuous gallantry."[73]

Many disgruntled citizens of the German states also came to the United States in the 1850s after their efforts to secure greater freedom in their native lands had failed. August C. "Theo" Ewert was one such immigrant. He left his native Prussia following the appointment of Otto von Bismarck as chancellor. A mere

THOMAS C. MURPHY *(Ireland), Illinois*

boy, Theo found employment as a butcher in Chicago. Just two months after celebrating his fourteenth birthday, in August 1861, he joined Thielman's Illinois Cavalry.[74]

Thielman's battalion fought their first battle at Shiloh, in Tennessee. They were then employed in Grant's first probes toward Vicksburg, Mississippi. By then Theo had come to the attention of his superior officers. In January and February 1863, he was assigned as orderly to the provost marshal of Memphis, Tennessee. While there he helped to enforce law and order in the occupied city. In June he transferred into Company B of the 16th Illinois Cavalry. A natural leader, he was with his regiment during the opening stages of the Atlanta campaign. When officers were needed for the many newly formed units of former slaves, Theo's colonel recommended him for a lieutenant's commission. On July 12, 1864, Theo became a second lieutenant in the 12th Light Artillery, U. S. Colored Troops. The seventeen-year-old relied on his own experiences as a young soldier to teach his men, many of them former slaves, their duties.[75]

AUGUST C. "THEO" EWERT (*Prussia*), *Illinois*

CHAPTER 12

The Ivy Leaguers

In New England abolitionist spirit ran high, and the sons of many distinguished families felt obligated to volunteer for military service. When the 20th Massachusetts Infantry needed officers, it chose two young university students. Oliver Wendell Holmes Jr. was the Harvard-educated son of a distinguished poet and physician. At twenty, he was approaching graduation when he accepted a first lieutenant's commission in Company A. William Lowell Putnam, another twenty-year-old, left Amherst College to join Company E as a second lieutenant. The two young men were to serve together only briefly.[76]

On October 21, 1861, at Ball's Bluff, near Leesburg, Virginia, both young lieutenants faced a storm of Confederate rifle fire. Holmes went down first, struck in the belly by a spent bullet. Seeing himself unhurt, he regained his feet and charged onward. Putnam then received a mortal wound in his bowels. Assisted from the field, he died two days later in camp. Holmes, trying to reform his shattered company, was

WILLIAM LOWELL PUTNAM, *Massachusetts*

OLIVER WENDELL HOLMES JR., *Massachusetts*

then struck a second time. This time the bullet tore through one side of his chest and went out the other. The young man collapsed, believing himself mortally wounded.[77]

Oliver Wendell Holmes Jr. was destined for greater deeds, though. Promoted to the rank of major after Ball's Bluff, he eventually commanded his regiment as a full colonel. He was wounded again at Antietam, Fredericksburg, and Chancellorsville, but he survived. After the war was over, he returned to Harvard, graduated from law school, and ultimately went on to serve on the U. S. Supreme Court.[78]

In 1884, addressing a Memorial Day crowd, Holmes spoke for all Civil War veterans when he said:

> *You could not stand up day after day in those indecisive contests where overwhelming victory was impossible because neither side would run as they ought when beaten, without getting at least something of the same brotherhood for the enemy that the north pole of a magnet has for the south—each working in an opposite sense to the other, but each unable to get along without the other. As it was then, it is now. The soldiers of the war need no explanations; they can join in commemorating a soldier's death with feelings not different in kind, whether he fell toward them or by their side.*[79]

CHAPTER 13

A Future President

Eighteen-year-old William McKinley was hoping to resume his studies at Allegheny College in Meadville, Pennsylvania, the spring that the country went to war. His father's business was in trouble, though, so instead of attending college, young William was teaching at the local grade school and working as a post office clerk. When war fever spread through Ohio, William and his cousin Will Osborne of Youngstown decided to enlist. Despite McKinley's frail nature, the young man felt honor bound to join the ranks. The cousins made their way to Columbus, Ohio's capital city, and signed on with the 23rd Ohio Infantry.[80]

William found army life to his liking. He enjoyed the spirit of adventure. He made many friends among the other soldiers and soon caught the eye of the regiment's lieutenant colonel, Cincinnati lawyer and future U. S. president Rutherford B. Hayes. In a letter home Hayes described William as "a handsome, bright, gallant boy." Although the 23rd Ohio Infantry spent its early weeks rooting rebel irregulars out of the hills of western Virginia, it wasn't long before they saw their first hard fighting. The Ohio soldiers proved themselves by delaying Robert E. Lee's attacking

WILLIAM McKINLEY, *Ohio*

divisions at South Mountain in Maryland and standing firmly at Antietam. At Antietam William McKinley set himself apart by driving a wagon of hot food and coffee to his beleaguered comrades while shot and shell marked his path.[81]

Although McKinley's actions often appeared reckless, his private thoughts reflected a more serious side. In his diary the future president wrote of prayer meetings and friends. He described the rough country through which he marched and spoke of anxious moments spent on guard duty. On the eve of battle he recorded the feelings shared by many young Civil War soldiers: "It may be I will never see the light of another day. Should this be my fate, I fall in a good cause."[82]

After Antietam William won promotion to lieutenant. During a brief trip home, he proudly showed off his new officer's coat and shoulder straps. It was his last wartime visit. He remained with his regiment until he was assigned to the quartermaster's bureau. At Hayes's recommendation, he was promoted to captain. At war's end he was promoted major for "gallant and meritorious service."[83]

The Major, as McKinley liked to be called, became a lawyer and Republican politician. He was elected a congressman and served two terms as Ohio governor before running for president in 1896. During his first term, he oversaw the United States's victory in the Spanish-American War, a conflict he had tried to prevent. He won reelection in 1900 by what was then the highest popular majority ever received. While visiting the Pan-American Exposition in Buffalo, New York, on September 5, 1901, he was shot twice. Most expected him to recover, but he died four days later, the third U. S. president to die at the hands of an assassin.[84]

Assuming office was Vice President Theodore Roosevelt of New York. Roosevelt pledged "to continue, absolutely unbroken, the policy of President McKinley for the peace, the prosperity, and the honor of our beloved country."[85]

CHAPTER 14

The War at Sea

While armies were marching and fighting on land, hundreds of the Civil War's youngest participants were serving aboard ships on inland rivers or on the high seas. Life at sea could be both adventurous and brutal. Because most of the fighting took place in the South, conditions were a mixture of blazing summer days and fierce storms. The Civil War saw the first use of ironclad warships, vessels whose wooden sides were covered with iron plates. While such ships stood up well to the fire of heavy cannons located on forts or rival ships, life inside was often miserable. Southern ironclads, known as rams because of the sharp underwater projection used to smash holes in other ships below the water-line, were generally poorly powered. They often filled with thick smoke from blazing guns and broken steam pipes.

Life was little better aboard the famous Union monitors. These peculiar ships were the invention of John Ericsson, a veteran of the Swedish navy, who designed a shallow-draft iron-hulled vessel that would be able to navigate the nation's many rivers and inlets. Ericsson invented a revolving turret to hold the ship's twin heavy guns. After firing, the turret could be rotated to protect the gunners from direct

50

enemy fire. The guns could also be directed without turning the ship itself.

Monitors were small, cramped vessels, and their iron hulls and turrets could grow terrifyingly hot even when not in combat. Tight quarters forced most crews to sleep on deck. Sudden storms posed true peril as men were sometimes swept overboard. Monitors at sea were extremely unseaworthy. The original *Monitor* withstood the fire of the Confederate giant CSS *Virginia* only to sink off the coast in a gale.

While the United States Navy did important work transporting troops and supporting expeditions against Southern ports and key positions along the Mississippi River, the majority of the major ships established a blockade off the Southern coast in order to cut supplies from England and France. Blockade duty was often dull and monotonous, broken only by the exciting cat-and-mouse game played with sleek and swift blockade-runners. At first all kinds of vessels, from small sailing ships to captured naval vessels, attempted to sail past the patroling Union fleet. Later most blockade-runners were steam-powered iron-hulled ships built in Europe. They operated out of ports such as Nassau in the Bahamas. A single successful voyage through the blockade often paid for the price of a ship, and crewmen endured heavy risks and earned high wages. And because the crews of federal blockaders shared in the value of captured ships and cargoes, a successful chase could bring a rich reward.

It was quickly clear that the prewar U. S. Navy was ill-equipped for its many missions. Northern shipyards began turning out hundreds of new ships. The need for sailors was even greater. If army recruiters often turned a blind eye to the youthful appearance of their recruits, the shorthanded naval squadrons were desperate to fill their rosters. The navy welcomed black men aboard ship early in the war. Newly arriving English and Irish boys with experience aboard fishing craft were particularly welcome. Any veteran merchant sailor had his pick of assignments, and many won commissions as more and more ships were required to tighten and extend the blockade.

The Confederate navy faced even greater problems in building and equipping ships. With few manufacturing facilities and virtually no shipyards, they were forced to turn to innovative and makeshift solutions. Many of their most successful ships were purchased abroad, such as the famous raider *Alabama*, which captured or destroyed dozens of Northern merchant ships before being sunk off the coast of France. The first and perhaps best-known rebel ironclad, CSS *Virginia*, was constructed over the hull of the old United States Navy's *Merrimack*. Most of the blockade-runners obtained crews in foreign ports, but the gunboats and ironclads relied on veterans of the old navy supplemented by sailors whose ships were stranded in Southern ports because of the blockade. The CSS *Hunley*, the world's first successful submarine, was built from an iron tube that had served as the boiler for a steam engine. Even after two crews drowned during trials, daring young men volunteered for service aboard the experimental vessel.

The most common young sailors, though, were landsmen, inexperienced men who would be enlisted and trained while their ships were at sea. The more promising young landsmen received the rating of "ship's boy." One such youngster was Henry Messhage, who served with the Union blockading squadrons and is shown in the accompanying photograph carrying a powder sack. Ship's boys were sometimes called powder monkeys because they performed the vital role of carrying powder and shot to the waiting gunners. They soon developed a talent for walking barefooted on decks slippery with salt water. Ship's boys were also employed as personal servants of the officers and helped the ships' cooks prepare and serve food. They took rough duty in stride and performed well in the heat of battle.[86]

HENRY MESSHAGE, *First Class Boy*

CHAPTER 15

Mischief Makers

While many young soldiers got into hot water tormenting their elders with one prank or another, the champions at making mischief may have been a pair of young Wisconsin musicians. John Catlin and George Coleman were kindred spirits in the 28th Wisconsin Infantry. Johnny Catlin, from Delavan, Wisconsin, had drummed at town parades and political rallies. Although he was only twelve when the war began, he immediately enlisted in the 18th Wisconsin Infantry. He swelled with pride when he took his place in line for the first regimental inspection. The regimental colonel was a little startled to see the youngster, though.[87]

"Why, what in thunder is this?" he asked.

"That is our drummer boy, and he is a daisy," the captain replied.

The colonel didn't agree. "This is no kindergarten. We ain't running a nursery." Turning to Johnny, he told the boy to go home. "The war is no place for chickens that hain't got their pin feathers!"[88]

A disappointed Johnny tried next to sign on with the 3rd Wisconsin Cavalry, but again he was thwarted. He finally found his place with Company E of the 28th

Wisconsin Infantry on August 15, 1862. At fourteen, George Coleman was two years older. He had little difficulty gaining a place as Company B's drummer.[89]

The 28th Wisconsin spent its first months drilling. Then, in November 1862, they marched to Port Washington, Wisconsin. Citizens there had rioted when they heard the news that some of their neighbors would be drafted into the army. Once the armed soldiers of the 28th Wisconsin appeared, the citizens of Port Washington calmed down.[90]

The 28th Wisconsin Infantry faced its first heavy fighting at Helena,

JOHN CATLIN, *Wisconsin*

Arkansas, on July 4, 1863. Then, in February 1865, after two years of skirmishing with bands of rebels in Arkansas, they were dispatched down the Mississippi to participate in the land campaign against Mobile, Alabama.[91]

It was during the voyage down the Mississippi River that Johnny and George decided to enjoy a lark. Expecting that their regiment was on its way to New Orleans, the boys sneaked off their ship at the wharf in Vicksburg, Mississippi, and had a brief adventure touring the trenches and battered buildings of the town. By the time they finished exploring, their transport had sailed. Unconcerned, they boarded the next steamboat bound for New Orleans, expecting to join their regiment there.

Unfortunately the 28th Wisconsin continued down the Mississippi River and out into the Gulf. The startled drummers found themselves absent without leave hundreds of miles from their assigned post.[92]

The stranded youngsters were detained at a temporary camp, living on bean soup so thin "you had to dive to get a bean." From there they were sent to Dauphin Island, where they slipped away, evading musket fire while swimming to a safer spot along the beach. Finally they arrived at Fort Morgan and were reunited with their regiment.

As Catlin recalled years later:

GEORGE COLEMAN, *Wisconsin*

We were locked up in a cell and kept on bread and water for a few days. There was a large underground passage, it was very dark in there. Coming out of the fort one day, I thought I heard a voice that sounded like Col. Gray's, and on reaching the outside of the fort, whom did I find but our gallant Colonel. The first question he asked was, "Where is Coleman?" He always expected to find Coleman with me. I said, "He will be out soon." He then gave us a lecture, and said he thought the best thing he could do was to hang us. It was a dry, sandy country, and there were no trees within five miles, and we had the best of him on that point. The Colonel said we should be court-martialed—but the Colonel was always kind. The Colonel says, "Do you see that large steamer there at the wharf?" I says, "Yes, sir." "On that is the 28th Wisconsin. Now," he says, "we are going up above five miles from here, to Navy Cove, when you get time come up and see us. Good day."[93]

The boys wasted little time rejoining the regiment. Although they were treated to a number of taunts, they received no real punishment. "We remembered his once saying that we were only young boys," Catlin recalled, adding, "We never after that took advantage of his good nature." It was probably just as well because there were plenty of trees at Spanish Fort, where the 28th next saw action.[94]

CHAPTER 16

Boy Hero of the Confederacy

The Civil War wasted little time coming to Tennessee. Early in 1862, following the capture of Forts Henry and Donelson on the Tennessee and Cumberland Rivers, Northern armies occupied the capital city of Nashville. After the battle of Shiloh on April 6–7, 1862, Memphis fell. The south-central region witnessed bloody fighting at Murfreesboro (Stones River), Franklin, and Nashville. Confederates suffered bloody defeats on Missionary Ridge and Lookout Mountain near Chattanooga.

Like much of the Upper South, Tennessee was a state divided in its sentiments. Lincoln's second vice president, Andrew Johnson, claimed the state as his home. The Smoky Mountain region was strongly Unionist throughout the war. Even so, the principal western army of the Confederacy called itself the Army of Tennessee, and thousands of Tennessee men and boys served under the rebel banner.

While most young Tennesseans with Southern sympathies donned gray uniforms and fought in the line of battle, others chose a different means to serve their cause.

Samuel Davis of Smyrna was the eldest son of C. L. and Jane Davis. Only eighteen at the onset of war, he joined an irregular force under the command of Captain Henry Shaw. Shaw used the name Coleman when behind enemy lines, so his company became known as Coleman's Scouts. They were a thorn in the side of the thinly spread federal troops occupying the supply depots and small forts of central Tennessee. Coleman's men provided Confederate generals with information on troop movements,

SAM DAVIS, *Tennessee*

passed word of supply trains, cut telegraph wires, and created alarm and uncertainty. Eventually entire companies of Union cavalry were assigned the task of killing or capturing the scouts.[95]

Union General Grenville Dodge, who after the war became famous for constructing railroads through Kansas, was in command of the area around Pulaski, Tennessee. Determined to put an end to "Coleman" and his scouts, Dodge ordered cavalry units to patrol every principal road. He created a network of informants. In late November his agents came across a smiling, polite young man fifteen miles from Pulaski. He might have passed as a boy off one of the nearby farms but for the fact that he was carrying maps and letters detailing Union positions. General Dodge had caught one of Coleman's ablest scouts, young Sam Davis.[96]

Dodge took personal charge of the young man's interrogation. With the documents in hand, some of them stolen from Dodge's own headquarters, there was little doubt that Sam had been spying, or at least carrying dispatches from spies to army headquarters. Dodge confronted young Davis, who had just celebrated his twenty-first birthday the month before, with a difficult choice. Turn in his leader, Coleman, and ride safely home without interference, or be tried by a court martial as a rebel spy.[97]

Ironically, Captain Shaw was already a prisoner in the very jail where Sam was confined. Sam gave a simple answer, the one today inscribed on a memorial window in the Museum of the Confederacy in Richmond: "I would sooner die a thousand deaths than betray a friend or be false to duty." A Union witness to the hanging that followed, Lieutenant George Bargus of the 64th Illinois Infantry, spoke admiringly of the young spy, telling of how the boy offered to place the noose around his own neck to spare his executioners' feelings. "Such courage," Bargus wrote, "was worthy a Better Cause."[98]

In what must have been one of the most difficult duties of the war, Sam's sixteen-year-old brother, Oscar, accompanied a family friend to Pulaski to retrieve the body of his dead older brother. To Oscar's amazement, the federal soldiers greeted him warmly and spoke with admiration of his brother. As for General Dodge, he later told friends that he never slept peacefully again after the execution.[99]

CHAPTER 17

Caught in the Line of Fire

Not all casualties of the Civil War were soldiers on the battlefield. Armies clashed across farms and towns inhabited by civilians. Often innocent men, women, and even children were killed or wounded by rifle or cannon fire.

Mary Virginia "Jennie" Wade grew up in the crossroads town of Gettysburg, Pennsylvania. As a teenager she helped her mother and older sister mend torn garments or make alterations. At the outbreak of war, she was just eighteen. Often she helped her three little brothers and small sister with their school lessons. It was her nature to look after those in need, and when her married sister gave birth, Jennie moved in to help care for mother and child. When word came that Confederate General Robert E. Lee was marching with thousands of Confederate soldiers toward Gettysburg, Jennie's friends and neighbors fled. Her sister was unable to travel, though. Jennie would not leave her.[100]

As cannons boomed and lines of soldiers exchanged volleys, Jennie huddled with

MARY VIRGINIA "JENNIE" WADE,
Pennsylvania

her sister in the cellar. By the third day of the battle, the area around her Baltimore Street house was cluttered with Union wounded. Jennie left the safety of the cellar to help the injured and dying men. After bandaging wounds, she distributed all the food she had on hand among her uninvited guests. For most, that would have been enough. Many did less. Jennie Wade decided to bake fresh bread.[101]

Perhaps she was thinking of her childhood sweetheart, Union Corporal Johnston Skelly, who was with his regiment in the Shenandoah Valley of Virginia. Maybe she thought that by keeping busy, she could forget some of the horrors she had witnessed. Jennie was kneading dough when a stray bullet penetrated the wooden wall of her sister's house and struck her in the back. She died instantly.[102]

Ironically, Johnston Skelly had been mortally wounded just days before at Winchester, Virginia. Today they both lie in Evergreen Cemetery at Gettysburg, a short distance from where thousands of Union dead lie in the Gettysburg National Cemetery.[103]

CHAPTER 18

Left for Dead

James Philip Craver was born three days before Christmas 1844, in Georgia. His family had moved to Texas by 1860, and he was attending a local school in Marshall when the Civil War shattered his peaceful adolescence. He enlisted in Company D of the 32nd Texas Cavalry at Jefferson shortly before his eighteenth birthday. Although he envisioned a future filled with bold exploits and dashing cavalry charges, he found a far different life in the army. The 32nd Texas Cavalry was dismounted and performed its service as part of General Daniel Ector's infantry brigade in the Confederate Army of Tennessee. After fighting to little purpose outside Jackson, Mississippi, while the Union forces of General Ulysses S. Grant besieged and captured thirty thousand Confederate soldiers less than fifty miles away in Vicksburg, the regiment was heavily engaged at Chickamauga.[104]

J.P. saw his first hard fighting there. Ector's Brigade passed the winter at Meridian, Mississippi, where J.P. reenlisted. He accompanied his regiment to Georgia as part of Confederate General Joseph E. Johnston's effort to prevent the Union forces of General William T. Sherman from capturing Atlanta. The 32nd Texas Cavalry offered stiff resistance at Kennesaw Mountain near Marietta, Georgia,

JAMES PHILIP CRAVER, *Texas*

where J.P. received a severe wound through his right lung. Gasping for breath and bleeding, he was carried from the field. Surgeons removed a shattered rib, but they didn't expect the boy to live.[105]

Private Craver proved them wrong. He awoke during the night to find himself lying among the dead. With great effort he dragged himself to the surgeons' tent and called for help. He survived his wound to return home, marry, and raise thirteen children. He didn't die until June 25, 1906.[106]

CHAPTER 19

Storming the Fort

Michael Sowers was born in Pittsburgh, Pennsylvania, on September 14, 1844. His parents had come to the United States from Baden, in present-day Germany, hoping to find better opportunities. Unlike some boys in their teens when the war began, Michael waited until his eighteenth birthday had come and gone before enlisting. Then it was the promise of a $300 enlistment bonus, much of it provided by his neighbors in Birmingham Township, that lured him into the ranks of the 4th Pennsylvania Cavalry. In 1864 $300 could buy a farm, and a private's salary seemed a generous wage.[107]

Michael was an unlikely hero. Only five feet four inches tall, he spent most of his service raiding Confederate supply lines. It wasn't always easy duty. The Pennsylvanians often slept in the open, enduring rain and snow. On December 1, 1864, the regiment was ordered to attack a Confederate fort guarding the depot at Stony Creek Station, Virginia. Michael later described what followed:

We charged. All of a sudden my horse dropped forward on his knees to rise no more. That was the third horse killed under me within a short time, I was mad as a hornet and, resolving to make some rebels pay for this last loss, slipped off the back of the gallant little animal, took my Spencer and, running ahead of the encircling cavalry, made for the fort. Of course, I had no right to do that; but I was enraged and had but one object in view, to get even with those infernal Johnnies who were killing my horses. A lot of grape and canister came my way, but not close enough to injure me, so on I went right into the fort. I do not claim that I was the first to enter upon rebel ground—I was too excited to look about me. I do know, however, that I was one of the first, and that as soon as I was inside of the fort I emptied my gun into the rebels with telling effect.[108]

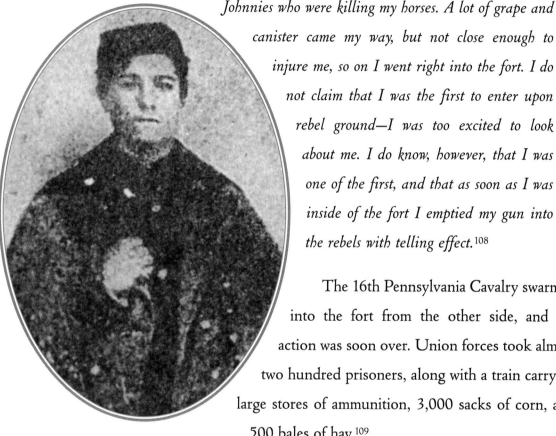

MICHAEL SOWERS, *Pennsylvania*

The 16th Pennsylvania Cavalry swarmed into the fort from the other side, and the action was soon over. Union forces took almost two hundred prisoners, along with a train carrying large stores of ammunition, 3,000 sacks of corn, and 500 bales of hay.[109]

On February 9, 1897, upon the recommendation of his regimental officers, the United States Army recognized Michael's bravery by awarding him the Medal of Honor for "most distinguished gallantry in action."[110]

CHAPTER 20

Alias George Tell

Frederick Gottlieb Uthoff was born February 3, 1845, in the Prussian province of Westphalia. After his father died, Fred accompanied his mother and older half brother to the United States in 1856. Before long they were in St. Louis, Missouri, where his mother, Henrietta Uthoff, remarried. The next several years were difficult ones for young Fred. As he tried to adapt to a new nation and learn English, he was constantly at odds with his abusive stepfather. When war broke out, Fred was working as a cigar maker in St. Louis. He saw enlistment in the army as a way to escape his tormented life.[111]

Perhaps nowhere was the Civil War fought as brutally as in Missouri. From the earliest weeks of war, neighbors chose sides and fought one another in small skirmishes from one end of the state to the other. On August 1, 1861, Fred joined the conflict. Perhaps fearful of being returned to his stepfather or discovered as being under the legal age of enlistment, Fred signed the muster book of the Union's 1st Missouri Cavalry as George Tell, age eighteen. He was assigned duty as Company E's bugler.[112]

Young Fred was present at every muster until April 1863, when he was permitted a brief visit home. The 1st Missouri Cavalry devoted most of its energy to fighting Confederate guerrillas, poorly organized groups of men who raided supply depots and terrorized Unionists in Kansas and southern Missouri. In the summer of 1863, the regiment took part in the capture of Little Rock, Arkansas. They were stationed in the Arkansas capital in December when Fred, alias George Tell, ran afoul of the law.[113]

The young bugler, encouraged by some of the older men, stayed out late celebrating the year's end and failed to report back to the regiment. He was arrested and confined in the Little Rock city prison. He remained there until May, when his company commander, A. D. Mills, interceded with authorities.[114]

Captain Mills wrote:

Sir:

I have the honor to ask that you will release from the city prison, George Tell, a bugler of my company.

He has been confined four months, under charges, awaiting court martial, and I learn today that he is quite sick.

He is but a boy, and has been an excellent soldier, and would never have committed the act for which he is confined if he had not been lead astray by older heads.

If you will have the goodness to release him on parole, I will hold myself responsible for his appearance at any time you may call for him.[115]

Captain Mills's words had immediate effect, and Fred was released to his company commander. Mills, seeing the poor condition of his young bugler's health, assigned the boy to nursing duty at the regimental hospital for the remainder of the summer.

FREDERICK GOTTLIEB UTHOFF *(Prussia), Missouri*

On September 17, 1864, George Tell was honorably discharged from the United States Army at St. Louis.[116]

Fred continued to serve his state and nation after the war. He won election as a city alderman in St. Louis, but scandal spoiled his political career. He journeyed to Leadville, Colorado, where he had a successful career in the mining industry. When he applied for a veteran's pension, he finally set the record straight. A pension was granted to Frederick Gottlieb Uthoff, "alias George Tell."[117]

CHAPTER 21

Battle Cry of Freedom

No group of Americans had as much at stake in the outcome of the Civil War as those held in bondage. Although the United States Declaration of Independence announced to the world that "all men are created equal," victory over the British did not bring freedom to all Americans. Slavery was still recognized in the Southern states long after 1776. Even when Abraham Lincoln issued his famous Emancipation Proclamation on September 22, 1862, slaves in the border states of Missouri, Kentucky, Maryland, and Delaware were not affected. Only slaves held in regions of the South still in rebellion on January 1, 1863, were freed under the proclamation.[118]

As Union armies penetrated large areas of the South, many slaves left their owners, hoping to find freedom in the federal army camps. Others hoped to join the fight. Spurred by orators such as the fiery former slave Frederick Douglass, many Northern citizens began favoring the idea of enlisting black soldiers in federal regiments. Former slaves had contributed to the Union cause as cooks, hospital attendants, and laborers. The navy had welcomed blacks as crewmen from the opening days of the war. Finally, in July 1862, the U. S. Congress passed a militia

before   *after*

"DRUMMER JACKSON," *Kansas*

bill authorizing the enlistment of "persons of African descent" for all military purposes, including active service in the ranks of the army.[119]

One early black regiment was the 1st Kansas Colored Infantry Regiment, a unit formed of escaped slaves and free blacks. On April 18, 1864, at the battle of Poison Spring, Arkansas, the 1st Kansas Colored Infantry fought defiantly in defense of a Union supply train after other units ran. The unit suffered fearful losses, but the men won the respect of enemy and friend alike.[120]

In the above often-published "before and after" photographs, a young black man known simply as Drummer Jackson is shown in the rags of bondage as well as in the neat new uniform of the U. S. Army. The strong propaganda value of such pictures prompted numerous photographers to visit the enlistment camps of the newly organized black regiments. Sometimes photographers would carry ragged remnants of clothing in their wagons for the recruits to wear while photographed. Actually, the picture on the right was probably taken first. Then, after the soldier changed clothes, the "before" photograph would be made. It was an effective technique, but the youngster's well-groomed hair and clean physical appearance stand in stark contrast to those photographs taken in Southern cotton fields or in Union army camps where escaping slaves were often detained by military authorities.

The 79th U. S. Colored Infantry was formed from the 1st Kansas Colored Infantry on December 13, 1864. Its men served ably in Arkansas, remaining there at the close of the war as part of the military occupation of the South. Five officers and 183 enlisted men from the regiment were killed or mortally wounded in combat. An additional officer and 165 enlisted men died of disease prior to the men's eventual discharge on October 30, 1865, at Fort Leavenworth, Kansas. The heavy losses reflected the determination of this early black regiment to prove the worth of soldiers of African descent.[121]

Another early black regiment formed during the Civil War was the famous 54th Massachusetts Infantry. Frederick Douglass himself took an active interest in the raising and assignment of the unit. The governor of Massachusetts, John A. Andrew, invited a young captain from the 2nd Massachusetts Infantry, Robert Gould Shaw, to command the new regiment. The first recruits, most of them free blacks who were born and raised in the North, assembled at Readville, Massachusetts, in March 1863. During a rigid inspection, nearly one third of the volunteers were rejected. Only the ablest men were accepted. The officers, most of them sons of prominent Boston families, were young white men in their late teens and early twenties. The regiment was mustered into service on May 13, 1863, and shortly thereafter newly promoted twenty-five-year-old Colonel Shaw led them aboard a transport for the trip south.[122]

Among the youngest soldiers aboard the southbound steamer was Charles Miles Moore of Elmira, New York. The fifteen-year-old coachman had journeyed all the way to Massachusetts in order to join the army. Just five feet tall, Miles managed to talk his way onto the muster roll as drummer for Company H. Although he had spent his life in a free state, Miles was as determined as anyone that the 54th Massachusetts give a good account of itself at the earliest opportunity.[123]

CHARLES MILES MOORE,
Massachusetts

When the regiment landed at Port Royal, South Carolina, the men marched off, hoping for an early taste of combat. Instead they were assigned duty building or improving fortifications. On July 16, while scouting nearby James Island, they finally got their first taste of battle. A dawn attack by rebel soldiers of the 25th South Carolina Infantry broke the 54th Massachusetts's line. Rather than turn and run, though, the 54th rallied and stubbornly held its ground until reinforcements could arrive.[124]

The success of the 54th Massachusetts Infantry on James Island earned it a chance for glory two days later. For months federal forces had been making gradual progress toward the heart of Confederate territory, the port city of Charleston, South Carolina. The key to the land approach via Morris Island was a strong earthwork fort, Battery Wagner. The 54th Massachusetts was given the honor of leading the attack on the powerful Confederate position. Miles Moore was with Company H on the left flank of the second wave. As the sun set, a sea fog rolled in, and the men started forward. Calmly, steadily, the lines marched toward the waiting Confederates. Once spotted, the rebels fired their cannons and opened up a withering fire with rifles. The Massachusetts line shuddered under the heavy fire, but with their gallant colonel leading the way, they rushed onward. Reaching the parapets, they fought the Confederate defenders hand to hand. In clusters of five or six and later singly, they held their ground until one by one they fell wounded or dying. Young Miles and the other drummers helped the wounded to the rear. It was impossible to see clearly in the darkness, and most of the officers had been killed or wounded. The regimental colors were torn from their staff and lost. When reinforcements failed to arrive, the survivors of the attack finally retreated, leaving the Confederates holding their fort.[125]

The attack on Battery Wagner, portrayed in the 1989 motion picture *Glory*, won the 54th Massachusetts undying fame. It also thinned the regiment's ranks. Colonel Robert Gould Shaw lay dead on the field. Two other officers were killed, and 11 others were wounded. Of slightly fewer than 600 enlisted men, 31 were killed, 135 were wounded, and 92 others were taken prisoners of war.[126]

Miles Moore survived the terrible slaughter at Battery Wagner to continue his service with the 54th Massachusetts. Except for a brief period on detached service and a short confinement in May 1865, he was on active service during every campaign of his regiment. He finally completed his service on August 20, 1865, and was mustered from service at Charleston, where the war had begun four years earlier.[127]

Before the end of hostilities in 1865, more than a hundred regiments were formed to accept more than two hundred thousand black recruits and seven thousand white officers. Four out of five of these men had been slaves before the war. To serve as officers, the U. S. Army recruited outstanding young white soldiers, often from the enlisted ranks, promising them rapid promotion and better pay. Because the black regiments were often assigned the job of manning supply depots or guarding isolated railroads, some white soldiers who had seen heavy action in Virginia, Tennessee, or Georgia may have found the notion of rear area service appealing. Others, such as Robert Gould Shaw and like-minded young men, accepted command of regiments because they believed in racial equality.

Henry Campbell was only sixteen years old on July 12, 1862, when he enlisted in Captain Eli Lilly's 18th

HENRY CAMPBELL, *Indiana*

Indiana Light Artillery. He had been refused enlistment until Captain Lilly, at age twenty-four a veteran of the war's early campaigns, accepted the young clerk from Crawfordsville as the battery's bugler. After a few days of drill, Henry made a brief visit home. When he returned to his battery, he felt uneasy. "Left home forever," he later wrote. "Never expected to live through the hardships." When a surgeon inspected the recruits in August, Henry was again deemed too young for military service. Once more Captain Lilly stepped in, arguing that it was "essential to the interests of the service" that Henry serve as company bugler.[128]

After a year and a half of duty with the artillery, Henry obtained a commission as second lieutenant in the 101st U. S. Colored Infantry. The regiment protected the critical Louisville and Nashville Railroad from rebel raiders. Following Confederate General Robert E. Lee's surrender, most of the Union regiments were sent home, but the 101st U. S. Colored Infantry remained on active duty in Tennessee until January 1866. Although Henry's family urged him to resign and return home to prepare for college, he stayed with the regiment. "I don't think I could confine myself long enough to learn a lesson," he wrote. "After so much roaming around it is going to take some time to get settled down."[129]

During the final months of the war, there were more soldiers serving in units of the U. S. Colored Troops than in all the Southern armies then in the field. Despite the fact that they were often denied the chance to participate in actual combat, the casualty statistics reveal much about their service. Black regiments suffered approximately the same percentage of men killed in combat as in white regiments. Adding in those men who died of disease and accident, black soldiers died twice as often as those serving in white units. Oddly, black soldiers were only half as likely to be absent in hospital. Of the thousands serving the Union cause, hundreds chose to remain in the army after the war. They served equally well in frontier infantry and cavalry service.[130]

Side view of the African-American Civil War Memorial, Washington, D.C.

CHAPTER 22

Boys No Longer

The Civil War saw many positive advances in medical care and technology. Even so, deaths by illness far exceeded all battlefield losses, and the necessity of moving large numbers of men across great distances made change necessary. The ability of both Union and Confederate governments to adapt to new problems was at times remarkable. In one area, though, both sides shared common shortcomings—the care of prisoners taken on the battlefield.

During the war's first two years, most prisoners were simply paroled following a short period of confinement. Although housing and feeding large numbers of enemy soldiers posed problems, most prisoner deaths were due to battlefield wounds or diseases such as measles and pneumonia that were as common in regimental camps as in prisons. From the beginning the exchange cartel, as it was called, caused problems. The idea was simple enough. Representatives of the opposing governments brought records of how many soldiers had been paroled to a predetermined location. Privates counted as one man. Corporals, sergeants, and officers counted more. A general could return to action if another general was exchanged, or he might be "exchanged" for a hundred privates.

Both sides were suspicious of the other side's record keeping. Soldiers who were paroled on the battlefield rather than sent to prison camps often returned to action immediately or went home. They were often overlooked during meetings of the cartel. An additional problem was the use by the Union army of former slaves. In many Southern states, these men were considered criminals and subject to execution or return to their masters. When U. S. Grant took command of all Union armies in 1864, he argued that the exchange unfairly benefited the Confederacy. Freed Union prisoners often returned home or passed the remainder of their enlistments in hospitals. Confederates, on the other hand, returned to the ranks.

At Grant's urging, the Union withdrew from the cartel. Suddenly both sides were faced with thousands of prisoners. The old prison camps, often suitable for brief imprisonment, offered little or no shelter and poor medical attention. While there were instances of intentional neglect and even cruelty on both sides, most of the suffering was the result of long confinement in close quarters and the inability, especially by the South, to provide sufficient food, shelter, and medical care for its captives.

Confederate Henry Howe Cook enlisted as a private in Company D of the 1st Tennessee

HENRY HOWE COOK, *Tennessee*

Infantry Regiment in the opening hours of the war. Just sixteen, he quickly rose to the rank of second lieutenant in the new 44th Tennessee Infantry. During the heated fighting at Murfreesboro, Tennessee, on December 31, 1862, he was wounded in the hand and sent to Marietta, Georgia, to recover. His brother William lost an arm in the same battle and was taken prisoner by Union forces. By September 1863, though, William had returned home and Henry was back with his regiment, commanding Company I during the bitter fighting at Chickamauga. In May of the following year he was captured outside Richmond, Virginia.[131]

In August he was sent with a group of fellow officers to Fort Pulaski, Georgia, where he was placed in the line of fire in response to a similar ploy by Confederate officials. Both sides agreed to cease using prisoners to deter enemy operations, and Henry was ushered aboard a transport and sent to Fort Delaware, built on an island in the Delaware River to guard the approach to Philadelphia.[132]

Perhaps it was the hazardous exposure to the gunfire of his own comrades in Georgia that caused Henry to lose heart. Federal forces had occupied his home state, and the South was clearly losing the war. The damp, insect-infested conditions at Fort Delaware were adding friends to the sick list each day, and many never returned from the post hospital. Following Lee's surrender and the assassination of Abraham Lincoln, Henry wrote new president and fellow Tennessee native Andrew Johnson personally:

I joined the C. S. Army when I was 16 years old, being persuaded to do so by those older than myself after due consideration, being more mature in years, I am willing and anxious to return home and live a peaceable life. As a Tennessean I respectfully ask you to permit me to take the oath of allegiance and to send me home.

GEORGE ALBERT TOD, *Iowa*

Henry's request was granted, and he left Fort Delaware on June 16, 1865. He proved himself a dutiful citizen, practicing law and eventually rising to the position of chancellor of the state court system.[133]

George Albert Tod was only sixteen when he left his home in Webster County, Iowa, to sign up with the 32nd Iowa Infantry. He was assigned as drummer for Company I. The five-foot-tall drummer won the hearts of his comrades by his diligent service and cheerful attitude. Accustomed to hard work in his father's sawmill, George never let his size or the weight of his duties discourage him. While the other men were busy drilling or making camp, he would often set off to locate a stray hog or chicken to supplement the bland provisions provided by the army.[134]

George and his fellow soldiers were with General William T. Sherman's army when it moved toward the key Confederate supply base at Meridian, Mississippi, in early 1864. On February 4, George was caught by a group of Confederate scouts and taken prisoner. The seventeen-year-old soon found himself within the stockade of a new Confederate prison, Camp Sumter, at Andersonville, Georgia. George's parents were heartbroken. No one knew what had become of their son. In desperation Samuel Tod wrote his son's commanding officer, "If you can give me any information concerning him you will much oblige a sorrowing family."[135]

Had the Tods known their son's dire circumstances, they would have been even more concerned. In the ten months in which Union soldiers were kept at Camp Sumter, almost a third of the prisoners died. George complained that "the starvation and torture more than equaled the most vivid imagination of hell." George's solution was to escape. On July 26, 1864, he ran away from a work party. Friendless and without a map or compass, he was unable to make his way north. On August 10 he was recaptured, returned to Andersonville, and placed in irons.[136]

George wasn't there for long, though. Following the fall of Atlanta in September, Union prisoners were moved north. Near Charleston, South Carolina, George escaped again. This time he evaded Confederate authorities. Eventually he joined a party of paroled prisoners and arrived at Camp Parole in Annapolis, Maryland. On Christmas Day, 1864, he was furloughed home. When he arrived at his parents' home on January 1, 1865, his sister Mary was shocked to realize the walking skeleton was her big brother. George was suffering from scurvy, yellow fever, and malnutrition.[137]

The eighty-day furlough allowed Andersonville survivors was extended by an army surgeon, who noted George was suffering from "general debility and prostration" brought about by his long confinement. George finally returned to his regiment in July 1865. A few days later, after collapsing while on duty, he was finally discharged.[138]

WILLIAM F. CLARKE, *Connecticut*

CHAPTER 23

Eighteen Wounds

Some of the most exciting exploits of the Civil War were performed by small bands of Union and Confederate cavalry. Southern General John Hunt Morgan led his Kentucky and Tennessee horsemen across the Ohio River and spread panic through Ohio and Indiana before being trapped and made a prisoner of war. Union Generals George Stoneman and Benjamin Grierson launched raids deep into Southern territory, disrupting Confederate troop movements and destroying key bridges and railroads. Perhaps the most dangerous cavalry leader of the war was Nathan Bedford Forrest, a former Memphis slave broker, who repeatedly evaded superior federal forces and captured isolated groups of soldiers and supply depots.

William F. Clarke, a private in Company A of the 1st Connecticut Cavalry and a native of Peterboro, New Hampshire, was one of the young soldiers who followed Union General James H. Wilson toward the vital Confederate depot at Danville, Virginia, in June 1864. Already a veteran soldier, William had come a long way from his prewar days as a teenage clerk in Hartford, Connecticut. William's willingness to charge recklessly toward the enemy made him a good cavalryman, but it almost ended his life that summer. Wounded on June 28 at Reams' Station in Virginia and again the following day at Stony Creek Station, William insisted on remaining with his regiment. On June 30, while the raiders were returning from their assault on the Confederate supply bases, William was shot a third time from ambush.[139]

This time he was unable to remain in the saddle. Weak from loss of blood, he fell from his horse and was captured by rebel irregulars. Rather than bandage his injured shoulder, his captors took William's weapons, equipment, and supplies. When William objected, they turned and shot him fifteen times! Had not regular Confederate soldiers arrived, he would certainly have died. Instead, bandaged and carried to the nearby depot, William Clarke was on his way to a prison camp. Amazing as it may sound, this young man, with one arm nearly useless and his body pierced by eighteen gunshot wounds, managed to slip away on the night of July 3. He celebrated Independence Day as a free man back within Union lines.[140]

William spent the next eight months in hospitals, undergoing surgery and recovering from his various wounds. He returned to his regiment in March 1865, but surgeons determined he was unfit for the rigors of cavalry service and ordered him discharged on May 29, 1865. He recovered from his wounds and was still living and sharing the tale of his battle with guerrillas when he sent the photograph on page 82 to General John Logan in January 1888. Clarke's eighteen wounds, all received in a three-day period, have to stand as a record for Civil War soldiers.[141]

CHAPTER 24

"Put the Boys In"

The Virginia Military Institute at Lexington in the Shenandoah Valley was one of the finest military schools in the South. The legendary Stonewall Jackson, hero of the War with Mexico and future Confederate general, had taught there before the war. Its graduates led regiments and brigades throughout the Civil War. Following the breakdown of the prisoner exchange, the Confederacy grew desperately short of soldiers. Even after conscription officers drafted every able man in sight, there were not enough men to guard the Shenandoah Valley from the expected Union attack in the spring of 1864.

At VMI a few hundred cadets aged fourteen to eighteen studied military tactics and prepared for the day when they would lead men in battle. They were armed and equipped, well disciplined, and eager to join their fathers and brothers in the defense of their country. Before 1864, a cadet from time to time had left school to join the army, but most concentrated on their studies and waited for a chance to prove their worth. It came on May 15, 1864, at the sleepy little town of New Market, Virginia.

The importance of the Shenandoah Valley was recognized in the earliest days of the war. It provided a natural invasion route northward toward Washington or southward into the heart of Virginia. To the South it was Stonewall Jackson's valley, birthplace of one of their greatest heroes and the site of the general's greatest triumphs. The Valley, sometimes called the breadbasket of Virginia, provided vast quantities of crops and livestock for rebel armies. Its seizure would spell the beginning of the end for Robert E. Lee's Army of Northern Virginia.

On May 2, 1864, Lee wired Francis H. Smith, VMI superintendent, that he should inform General John C. Breckinridge, Confederate commander in the Valley, that the cadets were available for service. The approximately two hundred fifty boys and their two artillery pieces provided little comfort for Breckinridge. The former U. S. vice president and runner-up to Lincoln in the election of 1860 faced Union General Franz Sigel's invading force of some nine thousand Union soldiers and twenty-eight cannons with half as many men.[142]

Breckinridge didn't want the cadets in his army, and he certainly didn't want them to play a key part in the coming fight. They were, for all their training, just

JAQUELINE BEVERLY STANARD, *Virginia*

schoolboys. He assigned them a place in the rear, as far from the front line as possible. While veterans shouted jests at the youngsters, the boys themselves prepared for battle. As Union formations pressed Breckinridge's fragile line, spreading his regiments thinly across a wide front, a gap appeared in the rebel center. With a heavy heart, Breckinridge sighed and gave the fateful order. "Put the boys in," the general ordered, "and may God forgive me for the order."[143]

WILLIAM HENRY CABELL, *Virginia*

The cadets marched forward. No one held back. In fact, young Beverly Stanard, ordered to stay behind with the wagons, raced forward to be with his friends. At first things went well for the Union army, but as the Confederates broke the Union line elsewhere, the cadets charged the center. Amid a fearful clatter of rifle fire, Union batteries opened up. One shell exploded in front of William Cabell, a cousin of the commanding general. Cabell fell to the ground, writhing in agony.[144]

SAMUEL ATWILL,
Virginia

NICHOLAS JAMES BAYARD,
Georgia

The advance did not slow. Cadet William McDowell dropped to his knees after a bullet tore through his heart. "The fire was withering," Scott Ship, the cadet's young commander, recalled. "It seemed impossible that any living creature could escape."[145]

Beverly Stanard, the boy who wouldn't stay behind, fell with a broken and mangled leg. Moments later Thomas Garland Jefferson, great-nephew of the former president, was hit in the abdomen. When friends came to help, Jefferson urged them onward. Samuel Atwill fell, wounded, as the attack continued. The cadets faltered only once, when Ship fell, struck by a spent bullet and temporarily stunned. Georgian Nicholas James Bayard urged his friends ahead, and the survivors raced on. Finally they reached a rail fence. Pausing there to level their weapons, they opened a murderous fire on the enemy just ahead. The federal infantry then launched their own attack. When it was met with a storm of fire, the Union gunners prepared to withdraw their cannons.

It was time to make another, final effort. With a great shout, the cadets rushed forward once more.[146]

This time there was no stopping the charge. Dismayed, the federals turned and ran. The intense rifle fire had killed so many horses that not all the Union guns could escape. One cannon had to be left behind. The VMI cadets swarmed around their prize, shouting jubilantly and firing a few final rounds at the scampering enemy.[147]

It was a costly victory. After the smoke settled, Beverly Stanard was located. He had bled to death from his wound. Samuel Atwill appeared on the road to recovery, but he developed lockjaw and died July 20. For those who had missing friends or relations, the aftermath of the fighting was particularly painful. Sixteen-year-old Robert Cabell Jr. came upon the body of his brother William. Moses Ezekiel sat with his best friend, young Tom Jefferson, until Jefferson finally died on May 17. In all, nearly one in five of the cadets was killed or wounded.[148]

At VMI today, in the shadow of a monument titled *Virginia Mourning Her Dead*, stand the graves of six cadets killed or mortally

WILLIAM HUGH McDOWELL,
Virginia

MOSES JACOB EZEKIEL, *Virginia*

wounded at New Market. Samuel Atwill, Thomas Garland Jefferson, and William McDowell are among them. A memorial plaque pays tribute to others, including William Cabell and Beverly Stanard, who were buried elsewhere. The survivors of New Market remained in Confederate service. The school itself was burned a month after the battle when Union General David Hunter's forces occupied Lexington. Following the war, Nicholas Bayard returned to Georgia, where he led a quiet life prior to his death in 1883. Sir Moses Ezekiel became a leading artist. *Virginia Mourning Her Dead* is his tribute to fallen schoolmates. After years as a prominent European sculptor, he returned to create another monument dedicated to all Confederate dead. Ezekiel's own grave lies at the base of the monument, located at Arlington National Cemetery across the Potomac from Washington, D.C.[149]

THOMAS GARLAND JEFFERSON, *Virginia*

CHAPTER 25

Countrymen Once More

Four long years of war had left the Confederate States of America an exhausted nation of disillusioned people. Boys who had enlisted in 1861 had become old on battlefields from Virginia to New Mexico, from Florida to Pennsylvania. When the Union armies under the command of General Ulysses S. Grant trapped the remnant of Robert E. Lee's Army of Northern Virginia near Appomattox Court House on April 9, 1865, Lee knew that it was time to lay down his sword. Although some of his generals argued that the South could wage a guerrilla war in the hills and mountains, Lee knew such a fight would only lead to more death and destruction. He chose peace instead.

Alabaman Robert T. Coles was among Lee's veterans at Appomattox. Robert was an eighteen-year-old college student when he joined the ranks of the 4th Alabama Infantry on May 7, 1861. Two days later he was named sergeant major in Company F. The following March he won promotion to regimental adjutant with the rank of first lieutenant. Although wounded on June 27, 1862, during the fighting outside Richmond, Robert was soon back with the army. During hard fighting from 1863 to 1864, the 4th Alabama's ranks were thinned by death and disease. Robert himself was sick in Confederate hospitals during the summer of 1864. He was with his regiment during the final days of fighting in the Petersburg trenches and the frantic retreat that led to Appomattox Court House, though.[150]

Coles later recalled:

Though young in years, yet old in war's terrible experience, through which few have passed, these ragged, half-starved, grim-visaged veterans were almost heart broken. . . . The mortification of having to march up and stack arms in front of a host of men, whom we had every right to consider, man for man that we were their superiors, from past experiences on many battlefields, was most galling to our proud spirits.[151]

ROBERT T. COLES, *Alabama*

Also present at Appomattox was James Daniel Malone. He, too, was eighteen in May of 1861. James had been helping his two brothers on a farm outside Holly Springs, Mississippi, when war erupted. He enlisted as a private in Company G of the 17th Mississippi Infantry and participated in some of the fiercest fighting in the war. Except for a few weeks absent without leave in February 1863, he was with his regiment on every march and campaign. James survived four bitter years of fighting in the campaigns of the Army of Northern Virginia without suffering even a slight wound.[152]

JAMES DANIEL MALONE, *Mississippi*

Joshua Lawrence Chamberlain, a Union hero of Gettysburg and Petersburg who had recently been promoted to the rank of major general, recorded his impressions of the surrender:

They fix bayonets, stack arms; then hesitantly, remove cartridge-boxes and lay them down. Lastly—reluctantly, with agony of expression—they tenderly fold their flags, battle-worn and torn, blood-stained, heart-holding colors, and lay them down; some frenziedly rushing from the ranks, kneeling over them, clinging to them, pressing them to their lips with burning tears.[153]

As each regiment passed, the lines of Union soldiers on either side stood to attention. "General," said one of the defeated Confederates to Chamberlain, "this is deeply humiliating; but I console myself with the thought that the whole country will rejoice at this day's business."[154]

Perhaps a North Carolinian summed up the feelings of many:

I went into that cause and I meant it. We had our choice of weapons and of ground, and we have lost. Now that is my flag (pointing to the flag of the Union), and I will prove myself as worthy as any of you.[155]

Chamberlain himself, looking on as his men shared their rations with the starving rebels, observed:

We could not look into those brave, bronzed faces, and those battered flags we had met on so many fields where glorious manhood lent a glory to the earth that bore it, and think of personal hate and mean revenge. Whoever had misled these men, we had not. We had led them back, home.[156]

Homeward they marched, whether wearing blue or gray. The lucky ones found wives or sweethearts or mothers waiting. Too often, like Indiana's Henry Campbell, they found adjusting to life in a classroom or cornfield difficult at first. They were a remarkable people, those young veterans. They survived the hardships of war and the awful memories of slaughter to rebuild ruined homes, to explore new territory, and to serve their country again and again.

JUSTIN HARRIS, *Texas*

CHAPTER 26

Yesterday Is Today

The young men and women who fought and often died during the Civil War are long dead, but across the country bands of living historians are striving to bring their stories to life. Although the average reenactor is somewhat older than his wartime counterpart, the war's younger participants are well represented.

Fourteen-year-old Justin Harris has been interested in the Civil War since the third grade. When he read an article in the newspaper about the 9th Texas Infantry reenactors, he asked his parents if he could join. Although nineteenth-century shoes and clothing aren't always comfortable, especially in the heat of a Texas summer, Justin believes it is important to portray a Civil War drummer with as much historical accuracy as possible.

In his regiment, Justin is actually one of the older drummers. "The younger ones are about eleven," he explained. "We're getting a lot of interest in our fife and drum corps, so when I get a little older, I'll probably start carrying a musket."[157]

Since becoming a reenactor, Justin has experienced some of the hardships suffered by young Civil War soldiers. He has been hot and wet and weary. His avid interest has seen him through each difficulty. It has been contagious, too. He recruited his father into the regiment's ranks, and the two journeyed to Gettysburg for the 1998 reenactment. The 9th Texas Infantry was not present at that battle, so Justin played the part of a drummer in the 13th Alabama.

So long as young people remain interested in the stories of the youngest soldiers of the Civil War and living historians such as Justin portray their lives, they will not be forgotten.

Notes

[1] Wiley, Bell Irvin. *The Life of Billy Yank: The Common Soldier of the Union*, rev. ed. (Baton Rouge: Louisiana State University Press, 1978), 299; Wiley, Bell Irvin, *The Life of Johnny Reb: The Common Soldier of the Confederacy*, rev. ed. (Baton Rouge: Louisiana State University Press, 1984), 331.

[2] W. F. Beyer and O. F. Keydel, *Deeds of Valor* (Detroit: Perrien-Keydel, 1907), 35.

[3] *Ibid.*

[4] *Ibid.*

[5] C. W. Bardeen, *A Little Fifer's War Diary* (Syracuse: C. W. Bardeen, 1910), 17–19.

[6] *Ibid.*, 38.

[7] Delavan Miller, *Drum Taps in Dixie* (Watertown, N.Y.: Hungerford-Holbrook, 1905), 9–16.

[8] *Ibid.*, 107–9; 124–26.

[9] *Ibid.*, 149–50.

[10] USNA, Eighth Census, M563, roll 998; USNA, RG 94, Compiled Service Records of the 22nd Michigan Infantry.

[11] Greg Pavelka, "Where Were You, Johnny Shiloh?" *Civil War Times Illustrated* 27 (January 1989), 35–38.

[12] *Ibid.*, 40–41.

[13] Richard N. Current, ed., *Encyclopedia of the Confederacy* (New York: Simon & Schuster, 1993), vol. 1, 200; Belle Boyd, *Belle Boyd in Camp and Prison* (1865, reprint; Baton Rouge: Louisiana State University Press, 1998), 84.

[14] Boyd, *Belle Boyd in Camp and Prison*, 84–95.

[15] *Ibid.*, 104–7.

[16] *Ibid.*, 107.

[17] *Ibid.*

[18] *Ibid.*

[19] *Ibid.*

[20] USNA, Eighth Census, M653, roll 1317; USNA, RG 94, Compiled Service Records of the 3rd Vermont Infantry.

[21] *Ibid.*

[22] USNA, RG 94, CSR (3rd Vermont Infantry).

[23] *Ibid.*

[24] USNA, RG 94, AGO reports, Willie Johnston Medal of Honor File.

[25] *Ibid.*

[26] Robert G. Poirier, *By the Blood of Our Alumni: Norwich University Citizen Soldiers in the Army of the Potomac* (Mason City, Iowa: Savas Publishing, 1999), 48; National Medal of Honor Museum of Military History, Willie Johnston file.

[27] "On the March with Edwin Forbes," *Civil War Times Illustrated* 1 (October 1962), 17.

[28] United States National Archives, Eighth Census of the United States (1860), M653, roll 1353; USNA, Record Group 109, Compiled Service Records of Confederate Soldiers in Organizations from the State of Virginia, M324, rolls 246 and 443.

[29] USNA, Eighth Census, M653, roll 505; Edward E. Stanard, "Myron Philo Walker."

[30]Stanard, "Myron Philo Walker"; USNA, Record Group 94, Compiled Service Records of the 10th Massachusetts Infantry.

[31]*Ibid.*

[32]Stanard, "Myron Philo Walker."

[33]USNA, Eighth Census, M653, roll 691; USNA, RG 94, Compiled Service Records of the 3rd N. J. Infantry.

[34]United States War Department, *War of the Rebellion: Official Records of the Union and Confederate Armies* (1884–1924, reprint; Harrisburg, Pa.: National Historical Society, 1985), series I, vol. 25, part 1, 578.

[35]Frederick H. Dyer, *A Compendium of the War of the Rebellion* (Des Moines: Dyer Publishing, 1908), vol. 3, 1362–63.

[36]USNA, Eighth Census, M653, roll 332; USNA, RG 94, Compiled Service Records of the 31st Iowa Infantry.

[37]Steve Meyer, *Iowa Valor* (Garrison, Ia.: Meyer Publishing, 1994), 269.

[38]USNA, Eighth Census, M653, roll 421; USNA, RG 109, Compiled Service Records of Confederate Soldiers in Organizations from the State of Louisiana, M320, roll 106; Terry L. Jones, *Lee's Tigers* (Baton Rouge: Louisiana State University Press, 1987), 108–9. For years Jemison was mistaken for a Georgia soldier, Edwin Jennison. Many still list him at age seventeen. The 1860 census, taken almost exactly two years before, listed him as a twelve-year-old attending school in the Fourth Ward of New Orleans.

[39]USNA, CSR, M320, roll 106; Jones, *Lee's Tigers*, 109; Arthur W. Bergeron, Jr., *Guide to Louisiana Confederate Military Units, 1861–1865* (Baton Rouge: Louisiana State University Press, 1989), 75.

[40]USNA, Eighth Census, M653, roll 213; USNA, RG 94, Compiled Service Records of the 32nd Illinois Infantry.

[41]Wiley Sword, *Shiloh: Bloody April* (New York: William Morrow, 1974), 277–280.

[42]USNA, RG 94, Compiled Service Records of the 32nd Illinois Infantry; *Official Records*, series I, vol. 10, part 1, 103; Patton John file, Illinois State Historical Library, Springfield, Ill.

[43]USNA, Eighth Census, M653, roll 972; USNA, RG 94, AGO reports, John Cook Medal of Honor File; Beyer and Keydel, *Deeds of Valor*, 75.

[44]USNA, Eighth Census, M653, roll 1094; USNA, RG 94, Compiled Service Records of the 49th Pennsylvania Infantry; Robert S. Westbrook, *History of the 49th Pennsylvania Volunteers* (Altoona, Pa.: Robert Westbrook, 1898), 23, 124–26.

[45]Westbrook, *History of the 49th Pennsylvania Volunteers*, 124.

[46]USNA, RG 94, CSR (49th Pennsylvania Infantry); B. F. Clarkson (ed. by John M. Priest), "Vivid in My Memory: A Common Soldier and the Battle of Antietam," *Civil War Times Illustrated* 24 (December 1985), 25; Westbrook, *History of the 49th Pennsylvania Volunteers*, 23, 124–26: John W. Schildt, *Union Regiments at Antietam* (Chewsville, Md.: Antietam Publications, 1997), 102–3.

[47]USNA, Eighth Census, M563, roll 44; USNA, RG 109, Compiled Service Records of Confederate

Soldiers Who Served from the State of Arkansas, M317, roll 46; Bobby Roberts and Carl Moneyhon, *Portraits of Conflict: A Photographic History of Arkansas in the Civil War* (Fayetteville: University of Arkansas Press, 1987), 34, 215.

[48] *Ibid.*

[49] *Official Records*, series I, vol. 10, part 1, 488.

[50] CSR, M317, roll 46.

[51] USNA, Eighth Census, M562, roll 1292; USNA, RG 109, Compiled Service Records of Confederate Soldiers Who Served from the State of Texas, M323, roll 309.

[52] CSR, M323, roll 309.

[53] Charles D. Spurlin, ed., *The Civil War Diary of Charles A. Leuschner* (Austin: Eakin Press, 1992), 13.

[54] *Ibid.*, 13–15.

[55] CSR, M323, roll 309.

[56] U. S. Army Military History Institute, Henry Elms file.

[57] USNA, RG 94, Compiled Service Records of the 15th Illinois Infantry; *Waukegan Daily Sun*, August 29, 1899.

[58] USNA, RG 94, CSR (15th Illinois Infantry); Committee of the Regiment, *The Story of the Fifty-fifth Regiment, Illinois Volunteer Infantry, in the Civil War, 1861–1865* (Clinton, Mass.: W. J. Coulter, 1887), 43, 54, 467, 475, 480.

[59] Committee of the Regiment, *Story of the Fifty-fifth Illinois*, 43, 465; USNA, RG 94, Compiled Service Records of the 55th Illinois Infantry.

[60] Committee of the Regiment, *Story of the Fifty-fifth Illinois*, 237–38.

[61] *Ibid.*, 238–39.

[62] *Ibid.*, 239–40; USNA, RG 94, CSR (55th Illinois Infantry); USNA, RG 181, U. S. Naval Academy records, M991, roll 6; USNA, RG 94, Union pension file #199917.

[63] Committee of the Regiment, *Story of the Fifty-fifth Illinois*, 241; *Report of the Proceedings of the Association of the Fifty-fifth Illinois Veteran Volunteer Infantry at their Third Reunion held in Galesburg, Ill., Sept. 5 and 6, '88* (Davenport, Ia.: H. L. Wagner, 1889), 47.

[64] Burke Davis, *Gray Fox* (New York: Fairfax Press, 1956), 168.

[65] *Charleston News*, Feb. 6, 1880; "He Gave His Enemy Drink," *Civil War Times Illustrated* 1 (October 1962), 38–39.

[66] *Ibid.*

[67] "He Gave His Enemy Drink," 39; Les Carroll, *The Angel of Marye's Heights* (Columbia, S.C.: Palmetto Bookworks, 1994), 50–52.

[68] Carroll, *The Angel of Marye's Heights*, 63–65; "He Gave His Enemy Drink," 39.

[69] "He Gave His Enemy Drink," 39.

[70] USNA, RG 94, Compiled Service Records of the 30th Massachusetts Infantry.

[71] *Ibid.*; USNA, RG 94, Union pension file #475445.

[72] USNA, Eighth Census, M653, roll 216; USNA, RG 94, Compiled Service Records of the 31st Illinois Infantry.

[73] USNA, RG 94, CSR (31st Illinois Infantry).

[74] USNA, RG 94, Compiled Service Records of the 16th Illinois Cavalry; Illinois State Historical Library, A. C. Ewert file.

[75] *Ibid.*; USNA, RG 94, Compiled Service

Records of the 12th Light Artillery, U.S.C.T.

[76]Sifakis, *Who Was Who in the Civil War*, 315; USNA, Eighth Census, M653, roll 521; USNA, RG 94, Compiled Service Records of the 20th Massachusetts Infantry.

[77]*Official Records,* series I, vol. 5, 317.

[78]Sifakis, *Who Was Who in the Civil War*, 315; USNA, RG 94, CSR (20th Massachusetts Infantry).

[79]Richard A. Posner, *The Essential Holmes* (Chicago: University of Chicago Press, 1992), 80.

[80]Margaret Leech, *In the Days of McKinley* (New York: Harper & Brothers, 1959), 5–6.

[81]*Ibid.,* 6–7.

[82]H. Wayne Morgan, ed., "A Civil War Diary of William McKinley," *The Ohio Historical Quarterly* 69 (July 1960), 283.

[83]USNA, RG 94, Compiled Service Records of the 23rd Ohio Infantry.

[84]Leech, *In the Days of McKinley,* 17, 25, 595–602.

[85]*Ibid.,* 602.

[86]For a detailed study of life in the wartime navy, see Dennis J. Ringle's *Life in Mr. Lincoln's Navy* (Annapolis: Naval Institute Press, 1998).

[87]*Proceedings of Twelfth Annual Meeting of the Society of the 28th Wisconsin Volunteer Infantry held at Milwaukee, Wisconsin, June 13, 1894* (Milwaukee: King-Fowler-McGee, 1894), 50.

[88]*Ibid.*

[89]*Ibid.,* 50, 53; USNA, RG 94, Compiled Service Records of the 28th Wisconsin Infantry.

[90]Adam J. Kawa, "No Draft," *Civil War Times Illustrated* 37 (June 1998), 56–60.

[91]Dyer, *Compendium,* vol. 3, 1685.

[92]*Sixth Annual Meeting of the Society of the 28th Wisconsin Volunteer Infantry held at Milwaukee, Wisconsin, September 19th and 20th, 1888* (Milwaukee: S. R. Bell, 1888), 30.

[93]*Ibid.,* 30–31.

[94]*Ibid.,* 31.

[95]USNA, Eighth Census, M653, roll 1271; Sifakis, *Who Was Who in the Civil War*, 174.

[96]Sifakis, *Who Was Who in the Civil War*, 174.

[97]*Ibid.*

[98]"Eyewitness to Tragedy," *Civil War Times Illustrated* 18 (February 1980), 44.

[99]From information provided by the Sam Davis House, Smyrna, Tennessee. Sam's grave and the house in which he lived now form a permanent monument to his courage. A statue of Sam stands on the grounds of the Tennessee capitol in Nashville.

[100]USNA, Eighth Census, M653, roll 1057; Sifakis, *Who Was Who in the Civil War*, 680–81.

[101]Sifakis, *Who Was Who in the Civil War*, 681.

[102]*Ibid.*

[103]*Ibid.* The Jennie Wade House on Baltimore Street in Gettysburg is now a museum. It is one of the most popular stops on tours of the town and battlefield.

[104]USNA, Eighth Census, M653, roll 1296; USNA, CSR, M323, roll 156.

[105]USAMHI, J. P. Craver file; *Confederate Veteran* 15 (January 1907), 36.

[106]*Ibid.;* Texas State Library, Confederate Pension File 37545.

[107]USNA, Eighth Census, M653, roll 1065; Beyer and Keydel, *Deeds of Valor,* 465; USNA,

RG 94, Compiled Service Records of the 4th
Pennsylvania Cavalry.

[108]Beyer and Keydel, *Deeds of Valor*, 465.

[109]*Ibid.*

[110]*Ibid.*; USNA, RG 94, CSR (4th Pennsylvania
Cavalry).

[111]Constant E. Hopkins to author, July 7, 1998.

[112]USNA, RG 94, Compiled Service Records of
Volunteer Union Soldiers Who Served in
Organizations from the State of Missouri, M405,
roll 16.

[113]*Ibid.*

[114]*Ibid.*

[115]A. D. Mills to Provost Marshal, Little Rock,
Ark., May 18, 1864.

[116]USNA, CSR, M405, roll 16.

[117]Constant E. Hopkins to author, July 7, 1998;
USNA, RG 94, Frederick Uthoff pension file.

[118]Maryland abolished slavery by amending its
Constitution. The bill passed on June 24, 1864,
and was ratified by popular vote October 13 that
same year. James M. McPherson, *Battle Cry of
Freedom* (New York: Oxford University Press,
1988), 563, 706.

[119]Sifakis, *Who Was Who in the Civil War*, 189;
McPherson, *Battle Cry of Freedom*, 500.

[120]Frederick Dyer, *Compendium*, vol. 3, 1186–87.

[121]Dyer, *Compendium*, vol. 3, 1735.

[122]Luis F. Emilio, *A Brave Black Regiment* (Boston:
Boston Book Co., 1894), 2, 19–21, 31; Sifakis,
Who Was Who in the Civil War, 189, 584.

[123]USNA, RG 94, Compiled Service Records of
the 54th Massachusetts Infantry; USNA, RG 94,
Miles Moore pension file.

[124]Emilio, *A Brave Black Regiment*, 57–61.

[125]*Ibid.*, 72–79.

[126]*Official Records*, series I, vol. 28, part 1, 210;
Emilio, *A Brave Black Regiment*, 73.

[127]USNA, RG 94, CSR (54th Massachusetts
Infantry).

[128]USNA, Eighth Census, M653, roll 300;
USNA, RG 94, Compiled Service Records of the
18th Indiana Light Artillery; Henry Campbell,
"The War in Kentucky-Tennessee as Seen by a
Teen-Aged Bugler," *Civil War Times Illustrated* 2
(November 1963), 26.

[129]Henry Campbell, "Skirmishing in East
Tennessee, the Atlanta and Nashville Campaigns,
end of the war . . . and home," *Civil War Times
Illustrated* 3 (January 1965), 39.

[130]William A. Gladstone, *United States Colored
Troops, 1863–1867* (Gettysburg: Thomas
Publications, 1990), 119.

[131]USNA, Eighth Census, M653, roll 1279;
USNA, RG 109, Compiled Service Records
of Confederate Soldiers Who Served in
Organizations from the State of Tennessee, M268,
roll 297; Francis T. Miller, *Photographic History of
the Civil War* (New York: Review of Reviews,
1911), vol. 9, 311.

[132]USNA, CSR, M268, roll 297; Miller,
Photographic History of the Civil War, vol. 9, 311.

[133]*Ibid.*

[134]USNA, Eighth Census, M653, roll 345;
USNA, RG 94, Compiled Service Records of the
32nd Iowa Infantry.

[135]Dyer, *Compendium*, vol. 3, 1178; USNA, CSR
(32nd Iowa Infantry).

[136]USNA, CSR (32nd Iowa Infantry); USNA, RG 94, George Albert Tod pension file.

[137]USNA, RG 94, George Albert Tod pension file.

[138]USNA, CSR (32nd Iowa Infantry); USNA, RG 94, George Albert Tod pension file.

[139]USNA, RG 94, Compiled Service Records of the 1st Connecticut Cavalry.

[140]*Ibid.*

[141]*Ibid.;* Illinois State Historical Library, William L. Clark file. There appears to be some confusion over the actual spelling of Clarke's name. Although a William L. Clark did serve with the 1st Connecticut Cavalry, he was not the soldier wounded and captured during Wilson's raid on Danville. The Connecticut Adjutant General's reports and the compiled service records show this to have been Peterboro, New Hampshire, native William F. Clarke.

[142]William C. Davis, *The Battle of New Market* (New York: Doubleday, 1975), 26–28.

[143]*Ibid.,* 89, 121–22.

[144]*Ibid.,* 48, 122.

[145]*Ibid.,* 122.

[146]*Ibid.,* 132–37.

[147]*Ibid.,* 138–40.

[148]*Ibid.,* 159–61.

[149]James Gindlesperger, *Seed Corn of the Confederacy* (Shippensburg, Pa.: Burd Street Press, 1997), 144–45; VMI Archives, Alumni Records.

[150]USNA, Eighth Census, M653, roll 15; USNA, RG 109, Compiled Service Records of Confederate Soldiers in Organizations from the State of Alabama, M311, roll 120; Jeffrey D. Stocker, ed., *From Huntsville to Appomattox: R. T. Coles's History of the 4th Regiment, Alabama Volunteer Infantry, C.S.A. Army of Northern Virginia* (Knoxville: University of Tennessee Press, 1966), 9, 14.

[151]Stocker, *Coles's History of the 4th Alabama,* 193.

[152]USNA, Eighth Census, M653, roll 587; USNA, RG 109, Compiled Service Records of Confederate Soldiers Who Served in Organizations from the State of Mississippi, M269, roll 257.

[153]Joshua Lawrence Chamberlain, *The Passing of the Armies* (1915, reprint; New York: Bantam, 1993), 196.

[154]*Ibid.,* 200.

[155]*Ibid.,* 201.

[156]*Ibid.,* 205.

[157]Most of the information used in this segment comes from an interview conducted by the author with Justin Harris on June 14, 1998.

Glossary

abolitionist	a person who wanted to abolish slavery
blockade	the closing off of harbors and ports by patrols of enemy ships
blockade-runner	a vessel that attempts to penetrate a declared blockade by stealth or evasion
bounty	a bonus paid soldiers to encourage their entry into military service
cannon	a large brass or iron gun capable of hurling projectiles at ranges up to a mile or more
cartridge	a paper case containing powder sufficient for the firing of a musket ball or rifle bullet
cavalry	soldiers mounted on horses, usually used for scouting and raiding but occasionally dismounted and used as infantry in battle
confinement	usually a brief period of imprisonment for a minor offense
court martial	a military trial conducted by officers for violations of orders or army regulations
detached duty	brief assignment to brigade or corps formations, or to hospital or other support organizations
discharge	official release from military duty
enlistment	entry into military service by signing a muster, or enlistment paper
exchange	the official release of paroled prisoners of war to return to combat
garrison	troops assigned to defend a town or military post
guerrillas	men not carried on official army musters or acting under orders of the recognized government who engage in unofficial warfare
infantry	foot soldiers who fought with muskets or rifles, usually organized in regiments raised in local regions or by states
interrogation	official questioning, often of suspected spies or captured prisoners
ironclad	a warship with iron plate protecting some or all of its vital areas
irregulars	much like guerrillas (see above), loosely organized bands of men operating independently of official authority
muster	usually a bimonthly count made by a company of soldiers in a regiment

parole	the promise not to serve in active combat until officially exchanged
provost	military police official who enforced martial law and army regulations, especially in occupied territory
rebel	a person who opposes an established government
Shermanize	a term applied to the deliberate destruction of civilian and government property by the soldiers of General William T. Sherman, first during the Meridian campaign of early 1864 but especially during the march from Atlanta to the sea, September–December 1864.
siege	the process of surrounding and entrapping a fortified enemy force
substitute	a replacement paid to serve instead of a drafted soldier
truce	a temporary pause in combat, often arranged to allow the burial of dead or treatment of wounded following a battle

Select Bibliography

PRIMARY SOURCES

ARCHIVES

Illinois State Historical Library, Springfield,
Illinois:
William L. Clark File
A. C. Ewert File
Patton John File.
Massachusetts Commandery Collection. Military
Order of the Loyal Legion of the United
States. U. S. Army Military History Institute.
Carlisle Barracks, Pennsylvania.
National Medal of Honor Museum of Military
History, Chattanooga, Tennessee:
Willie Johnston File.
Texas State Library, Austin, Texas. Confederate
Pension Files.
United States National Archives. Eighth Census
(1860). M653. 1,438 rolls.
———. Record Group 94. Medal of Honor
Files.
———. Record Group 94. Compiled Service
Records of Volunteer Union Soldiers.
———. Record Group 94. Compiled Service
Records of Volunteer Union Soldiers
Who Served in Organizations from the State
of Missouri. M405.
———. Record Group 94. Union Pension Files.
———. Record Group 109. Compiled Service
Records of Confederate Soldiers in
Organizations from the State of Alabama. M311.
———. Record Group 109. Compiled Service
Records of Confederate Soldiers in
Organizations from the State of Arkansas.
M317.
———. Record Group 109. Compiled Service
Records of Confederate Soldiers in
Organizations from the State of Louisiana.
M320.
———. Record Group 109. Compiled Service
Records of Confederate Soldiers in
Organizations from the State of Mississippi.
M269.
———. Record Group 109. Compiled Service
Records of Confederate Soldiers in
Organizations from the State of Tennessee.
M268.
———. Record Group 109. Compiled Service
Records of Confederate Soldiers in
Organizations from the State of Texas. M323.
———. Record Group 109. Compiled Service
Records of Confederate Soldiers in
Organizations from the State of Virginia.
M324.
———. Record Group 181. U. S. Naval
Academy Records. M991.
———. Union Civil War Pension Files.
Virginia Military Institute Archives. Lexington,
Virginia. Alumni Records.
———. Cadet Records.

BOOKS

Bardeen, C. W. *A Little Fifer's War Diary.*
Syracuse; N.Y.: C. W. Bardeen, 1910.

Boyd, Belle. *Belle Boyd in Camp and Prison.*
Reprint. Baton Rouge: Louisiana State
University Press, 1998 (1865).

Chamberlain, Joshua Lawrence. *The Passing of the
Armies.* Reprint. New York: Bantam, 1993
(1915).

Committee of the Regiment. *The Story of the Fifty-
fifth Regiment, Illinois Volunteer Infantry, in
the Civil War, 1861–1865.* Clinton, Mass.:
W. J. Coulter, 1887.

Emilio, Luis F. *A Brave Black Regiment.* Boston:
Boston Book Co., 1894.

Miller, Delavan. *Drum Taps in Dixie.* Watertown,
N.Y.: Hungerford-Holbrook, 1905.

*Proceedings of Twelfth Annual Meeting of the Society
of the 28th Wisconsin Volunteer Infantry held at
Milwaukee, Wisconsin, June 13, 1894.*
Milwaukee: King-Fowler-McGee, 1894.

*Report of the Proceedings of the Association of the Fifty-
fifth Illinois Veteran Volunteer Infantry at their
Third Reunion Held in Galesburg, Ill., Sept. 5
and 6, '88.* Davenport, Ia.: H. L. Wagner, 1889.

*Sixth Annual Meeting of the Society of the 28th
Wisconsin Volunteer Infantry held at
Milwaukee, Wisconsin, Sept. 19th and 20th,
1888.* Milwaukee: S. R. Bell, 1888.

United States War Department. *War of the
Rebellion: Official Records of the Union and
Confederate Armies.* 128 vols. Reprint.
Harrisburg, Pa.: National Historical Society,
1985 (1884–1924).

Westbrook, Robert S. *History of the 49th
Pennsylvania Volunteers.* Altoona, Pa.: Robert
Westbrook, 1898.

MAGAZINES AND NEWSPAPERS

Charleston News. Charleston, South Carolina.
Confederate Veteran, 1895–1932.
Waukegan Daily Sun. Waukegan, Illinois.

LETTERS

A. D. Mills to Provost Marshal, Little Rock, Ark.,
May 18, 1864.

SECONDARY SOURCES

BOOKS

Bergeron, Jr., Arthur W. *Guide to Louisiana
Confederate Military Units, 1861–1865.*
Baton Rouge: Louisiana State University
Press, 1989.

Beyer, W. F., and O. F. Keydel. *Deeds of Valor.*
Detroit: Perrien-Keydel, 1907.

Carroll, Les. *The Angel of Marye's Heights.*
Columbia, S.C.: Palmetto Bookworks, 1994.

Current, Richard, ed. *Encyclopedia of the
Confederacy.* 4 vols. New York: Simon &
Schuster, 1993.

Davis, Burke. *Gray Fox.* New York: Fairfax Press,
1956.

Davis, William C. *The Battle of New Market.*
New York: Doubleday, 1975.

Dyer, Frederick H. *A Compendium of the War of
the Rebellion.* 3 vols. Des Moines: Dyer

Publishing, 1908.

Gindlesperger, James. *Seed Corn of the Confederacy.* Shippensburg, Pa.: Burd Street Press, 1997.

Gladstone, William A. *United States Colored Troops, 1863–1867.* Gettysburg: Thomas Publications, 1990.

Jones, Terry L. *Lee's Tigers.* Baton Rouge: Louisiana State University Press, 1987.

Leech, Margaret. *In the Days of McKinley.* New York: Harper & Brothers, 1959.

McPherson, James M. *Battle Cry of Freedom.* New York: Oxford University Press, 1988.

Meyer, Steve. *Iowa Valor.* Garrison, Ia.: Meyer Publishing, 1994.

Miller, Francis T. *Photographic History of the Civil War.* 10 vols. New York: Review of Reviews, 1911.

Poirier, Robert G. *By the Blood of Our Alumni: Norwich University Citizen Soldiers in the Army of the Potomac.* Mason City, Ia.: Savas Publishing, 1999.

Posner, Richard A., ed. *The Essential Holmes: Selections from the Letters, Speeches, Judicial Opinions, and Other Writings of Oliver Wendell Holmes, Jr.* Chicago: University of Chicago Press, 1992.

Roberts, Bobby, and Carl Moneyhon. *Portraits of Conflict: A Photographic History of Arkansas in the Civil War.* Fayetteville: University of Arkansas Press, 1987.

Schildt, John W. *Union Regiments at Antietam.* Chewsville, Md.: Antietam Publications, 1997.

Sifakis, Stewart. *Who Was Who in the Civil War.* New York: Facts on File, 1988.

Spurlin, Charles D., ed. *The Civil War Diary of Charles A. Leuschner.* Austin: Eakin Press, 1992.

Stocker, Jeffrey D. *From Huntsville to Appomattox: R. T. Coles's History of the 4th Regiment, Alabama Volunteer Infantry, C.S.A., Army of Northern Virginia.* Knoxville: University of Tennessee Press, 1996.

Sword, Wiley. *Shiloh: Bloody April.* New York: William Morrow, 1974.

Wiley, Bell Irven. *The Life of Billy Yank: The Common Soldier of the Union.* Revised Edition. Baton Rouge: Louisiana State University Press, 1978.

———. *The Life of Johnny Reb: The Common Soldier of the Confederacy.* Revised Edition. Baton Rouge: Louisiana State University Press, 1984.

ARTICLES

Campbell, Henry. "The War in Kentucky-Tennessee as Seen by a Teen-Aged Bugler." Civil War *Times Illustrated* 2 (November 1963), 26–29.

———. "Skirmishing in East Tennessee, the Atlanta and Nashville Campaigns, end of the war . . . and home." *Civil War Times Illustrated* 3 (January 1965), 36–39.

Clarkson, B. F. (ed. by John M. Priest). "Vivid in My Memory: A Common Soldier and the Battle of Antietam," *Civil War Times Illustrated* 24 (December 1985), 20–25.

"Eyewitness to Tragedy." *Civil War Times Illustrated* 18 (February 1980), 44.

"He Gave His Enemy Drink." *Civil War Times Illustrated* 1 (October 1962), 38–39.

Kawa, Adam J. "No Draft." *Civil War Times Illustrated* 37 (June 1998), 54–60.

Morgan, H. Wayne, ed. "A Civil War Diary of William McKinley." *The Ohio Historical Quarterly* 69 (July 1960), 272–90.

"On the March with Edwin Forbes." *Civil War Times Illustrated* 1 (October 1962), 12–17.

Pavelka, Greg. "Where Were You, Johnny Shiloh?" *Civil War Times Illustrated* 27 (January 1989), 35–41.

OTHER MATERIAL

Justin Harris interview, June 14, 1998.

Constant E. Hopkins to author, July 7, 1998.

U. S. Army Military History Institute. Carlisle Barracks, Pennsylvania. Audiovisual Department. James P. Craver File.

———. Henry Elms File.

Index